SNOW

lit rev

3

SPRING 2015

A·B

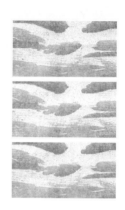

CEES NOOTEBOOM &
ANTHONY BARNETT

from

CORRESPONDENCE

Correspondence, selected from letters and cards written between 1998 and the present, is in manuscript, except for the first letter, which is typed, and emails. Minor amendments have been made, such as italicizing titles. In transcribing, intended unusual orthography, etc., has been kept as far as sensible. Elucidations follow an entry when it is felt they would be helpful. Bracketed ellipses denote omitted passages, which mostly concern incidentals or the tiresome vagaries of UK and US publishers.

———

Lewes, East Sussex   2 September 1998

Dear Cees Nooteboom

I wanted to write to you after reading *Roads to Santiago*, which I was drawn to for two reasons: my admiration for your novels and a visit to Madrid in March 1997. My friends took me one weekend to Medinaceli, which easily could have made a chapter in your book. Does the fact that it did not mean that you have not visited this town with its Moorish fort and Roman triptych arch? My little "obscure" prose piece enclosed mentions the result of my visit. I was struck by the immense irony of the memorial in the square to Ezra Pound, who wrote about cocks crowing there at dawn, and the Moorish belief (as I was told) that the Lost Ark of the Covenant was last seen there (if so that episode is missing from *Raiders of the Lost Ark*). The irony being that I envisage the Jewish Ark buried beneath the memorial to an anti-semitic poet . . . There is also what was once a synagogue in the town, but which became a church, and is now in disuse.

The rockrose (ref. my Blake question in the enclosed) is profuse in the wild round Madrid too. I keep this letter short, not knowing whether it will reach you or interest you. I hope it does. And my thanks for your books.

                              Sincerely

                         Anthony Barnett

———

The prose piece enclosed with the letter was a typescript of "Optical", first published in *Anti-Beauty* (2000 [in fact, 1999]), reprinted in *Poems &* (2012). In 2010, in response to my inquiring on a listserve about the Medinaceli Pound memorial, Andrew Brewerton responded by email: "Curiosity in this direction leads into dark waters. Describing the inauguration of this monument, the Chilean Nazi and 'esoteric Hitlerist' Miguel Serrano (a figure on the astral fringe of the postwar fascist international) says this was the question that Pound put to the Falangist journalist Eugenio Montes, who visited him in Venice, '¿Cantan aún los gallos del Cid al amanecer en Medinaceli?'" Many shifting references to Pound in Medinaceli, which he visited in 1906, can be found on the web, which were not available at the time of "Optical"and this letter. So, "Optical" is mistaken in attributing Pound's line to his writing, because he only spoke it.

———

San Luis, Menorca   Oct 8. 98.

Dear Anthony Barnett,

        O yes, I have visited Medinaceli, as I have visited Toledo, Cadiz, Cordoba – made extensive notes too, but then, at a certain moment, decided that enough was enough – which means of course that it never is, and that the book could have grown and grown.

But I must confess that I missed Pound's memorial (I saw his grave, and Brodsky's, and Stravinsky's last January in Venice) — and may make up for it on my coming short detour — leaving here tomorrow by boat and then driving via Medinaceli to Silos. The most correspondence I have received has been about Walter Muir Whitehill. Someone from Harvard sent me W's correspondence to his wife to be. The year is 1928, he travels with 9 suitcases, and tells her about the three monks (he lives then in Silos) that visit him in his cell, where they play cards and drink a 2 litres bottle of brandy more or less through the night!

Your letter, and the gloss on
Kundera & Bernhard etc. have
given me great pleasure.
Sincerely
Cees Nooteboom

———

Silos is an ancient Benedictine monastery. The gloss is in "Optical".

———

Lewes   27 November 1998

Dear Cees Nooteboom

I was very touched to receive a letter from you and to know that my letter about Medinaceli reached you safely.

I delayed writing again to you until I had received the Sun & Moon *The Captain of the Butterflies* which I had heard about and now have. [. . .]

I hope that you will not mind receiving the enclosed books. I would like you to have them and, given the way such things have to be published in England, it is unlikely that you would come to know about them any other way!

[5]

The Captain of the B is beautiful and it seems as if it is translated beautifully too – just from reading the English because I do not have your originals. But I do not understand what you say on p.13 about "gezicht". "Sight" carries all the meanings in English that you list, in varying degrees, & not just to a "poetic" ear. Eye Sight (as opposed to the "correct" "eyesight") carries all the meanings. You know, I do not accept the concept of untranslatability! If it is not asking too much: please read the interview with me in the enclosed book about my work – I talk a great deal about translation in there. (Of course, it is wrong of the UK publisher to have removed the word "detours" from anywhere on your title page, although I understand it is there as a sub-title in the USA.) Of course, too, I know that there are things for which we seem not to be able to find – to approach even – a translation. But, as I say in the interview: a good (& bad!) part, if not the whole, in some sense, of Western Civilization is based on a mistranslation of the Bible. And if we can accept that . . . Not that this is any justification for mistranslation – after all, it can lead to wars! But I do also enclose some of my translations – of the enclosed I do have reservations about my Vesaas – I have competely revised it and a new edition is scheduled to come out [. . .] perhaps in a couple of years.
    [. . .]
    Again, my apologies for such a pile of books but it is by way of thank you.
    [. . .]

with all good wishes
and hoping that you can decipher
my hand–(hard!) writing
Anthony (Barnett)

———

The Captain of the Butterflies (Sun & Moon, 1997) is a selection of Nooteboom's poetry. A larger, mostly different, selection is *Light Everywhere* (Seagull, 2014) in which Nooteboom and his new translator David Colmer do translate *Het Gezicht van het Oog* as *Eye Sight* and also use "The Eye's Sights"—see the two letters fol. The gloss on "detours" concerns the wrong titling of *Roads to Santiago* in English—for both points see also email, 29 April 2014.

———

Venice   16.1.99.

Dear Anthony Barnett,

            Nomad's life, mail forwarded, kept as company, not yet answered, but somehow answered – ah, I wish I could agree with you on translations, but I can, and cannot – having translated Borges (perfectly possible) Vallejo (god help us) – tried my hand on Gottfried Benn (failed with those incredible [. . .] rhymes) – same as Slauerhoff – who would ever be able to translate the non-existing damp-waas (a sort of condense at dusk rising from the
                                                              pampas
Slauerhoff, dutch sailor doctor poet, ships doctor on the Java–China– Japan line, 1898–1936 – one of our greats, but in tonality and bitter anti-musicality (I am sorry:) untranslatable. Yes, his meaning, but not his agonizing music. But we will talk about this later. Thank you for so many books. Zanzotto, yes, but so difficult, for me, to enter, but yes – and anyway, great admiration for <u>your</u> versatility.

I am packing – that is why all these things come to haunt me – they have travelled with me except your more voluminous book, which I must study, to get acquainted with your voice. No, I never discovered where Pound's line comes from, but stood there – one of those wild seeds sown in the middle of Spain, out of place, but for the gallos [. . .] – yes, in Spain they are everywhere but – Pound and Spain, ¿que?

[7]

From here I go to Provence – to stay with a chemical biofysical wizzard, Czech and American, who makes beautiful bibliophile books, then Holland, but only shortly. I must send you the dutch version of *Het gezicht van het oog* Zicht – Sight, o.k, but to get merchandise '<u>op zicht</u>' 2 words or talk about <u>menselijk opzicht</u>, in itself an untranslatable term, and yes, inzicht, but what about uitzicht, 1 word (= view) and zichtbaar: visible – meaning yes, but meanings <u>and</u> sounds – ? get the significance without the sound? Only rarely!

[. . .] But you are right – England is, alas, no fertile soil – for foreign writers/poets, and yet, the books you sent me are so beautiful, classic – do let me send you, something similar in Italian published by Crocetti – who also publishes, I think, Zanzotto. I hope you will like it.

All the best – forgive the hectic mood,
caravan when they breakup –

Cees Nooteboom

———

Pronunciation of "damp-waas" and "pampas" is the same. Czech—see email, 29 April 2014. Nooteboom sent *Autoritratto di un altro: Sogni dell'isola e dalla città d'un tempo* (Crocetti, 1998), a bilingual Italian–Dutch edition of *Zelfportret van een Ander*—see letter fol.

———

Lewes   4 February 1999

Dear Cees Nooteboom

[. . .]

It was very kind of you to respond to my packet of books – I was afraid that I had sent too much. And I am very grateful for your own work. Tomorrow I go to Paris, and then ten hours in the train to Berne and back in one day, with *Zelfportret* . . . and a little Dutch dictionary. I hope that by the end of that journey I will have read this <u>Dromen/ Sogni</u>.

When your letter & books arrived, my new little book enclosed was being printed. It includes the little piece I sent you before with the reference to Medinaceli, but this printing includes and epigraph by you quoted from *Santiago*. I hope very much that you will have no objection to my having done this – pp.26/27; note p.56. This is a strange book for me – the first time I have decided to print explanatory notes. And as will be clear, it is not all entirely serious – or is it?

Translation: yes, I think I am right and I am <u>wrong</u>. It is as if I <u>want</u> everything to be translatable . . . yet know that this is a tall order.

Zicht – sight/view: we do say such expressions as "out of sight (& out of mind!)"; "what a sight"; "a sight for sore eyes" and these mean "view" in some manner. This is too easy. I'm being reductionist.

You write in the margin of your letter: "caravan when they break up". Do you know the opening poem of Lagerkvist's *Aftonland*?

> Det är om aftonen man brytter opp,
> vid solnedgången.
> Det är då man lämnar allt.
>
> . . .

I have and have read several times four of your novels. *A Song of Truth and Semblance* is a book I often ask people to read, in this town, who [. . .] write novels. To ask them to consider some matters. There are many [. . .] novelists [. . .] in Lewes – perhaps because nearby is the village where Virginia Woolf lived and died!

[. . .]

With very best wishes
& hoping that 1999 is a
fruitful year of writing and travelling

Anthony

B.

———

Nooteboom's *Zelfportret van een Ander: Dromen van het eiland en de stad van vroeger* (1993) has twice been translated into English: by Duncan Dobbelmann as *Self-Portrait of an Other*, in *Grand Street*, 67 (1998); by David Colmer as *Self-Portrait of an Other: Dreams of the Island and the Old City* (Seagull, 2011). The large format Seagull edition includes the drawings by Max Neumann in the Dutch original.

———

Lewes   20 July 1999

Dear Cees

So you see, once again your book has entered into a piece of my own. Will you recognize the books of the other author that (mis)informs the piece? Almost certainly. But if not it is Paulo Coelho. You will gather a little of what I think of his books from this piece?
[...]
                                                        Sincerely
                                                                Anthony

———

The piece is "Lisa's Story"—see the two letters fol. Note also that it truly is something of an extraordinary coincidence that Lisa d'India happens to be a protagonist of Nooteboom's novel *The Following Story*.

———

San Luis   30.7.99.

Dear A·B.
                Thank you for "Lisa" and the letter; I like that idea of Lisa having a secret life outside me, and an evident intriguing conversational

acquaintance with you – though I must say that yes, I guessed which author you meant since I have glimpsed in his camino book as well – and understood why his camino does so much better than mine – but I would also say that Lisa is far too intelligent to like pseudo mystical eau de Cologne – Alas, it seems that world is taking over; three weeks ago I spent two hours in Santiago and fled. I will only return there when it freezes, snows, when tourist buses don't run and frost has chased all wishy washy sentiment away from the Pórtico de la Gloria: Imagine you are a real pilgrim – like my Italian publisher – She came walking all the way to an apotheosis of nada nada, a carousel of mass-nonsense. I could could only cure myself by driving into Trás-os-Montes, and then from Miranda do Douro along the whitest (on the map) most impossible roads that go right across the golden emptiness of the meseta, and through the maestrazgo mountains –

I liked the buddhist story – from time to time I read a page in *Two Zen Classics* Mumonkan & Hekiganroku – (N.Y., Weatherhill, 1977!) – Nansen Oshō saw monks of the Eastern and Western halls quarreling over a cat. He held up the cat and said "If you can give an answer, you will save the cat. If not, I will kill it." No one could answer, and Nansen cut the cat in two. That evening Jōshū took off his sandal, placed it on his head, and walked out. "If you had been there, you would have saved the cat", Nansen remarked. And then follows the commentary – and the questions for the poor pupils – scholastic casuistics, full of delightful nonsense, and always this idea that somebody knows what he is talking about, and you don't.

[...]

All the best,
Cees

———

[11]

San Luis   August 30.99.

Dear AB – Abi?   Thank you for "On the 31st of July" – you
certainly know how to make people either stupid or too intelligent –
so am I stupid to think that the title has to do that the 31st of July is
my birthday, or too clever by half. And what about Lisa? And AZ. Is
everything full of hidden ciphers, locks for which I do not have the
keys – like reading first Montale's poems and then be mystified (often,
underneath) and <u>then</u> read Arrowsmith's or Galassi's exegesis – and
enter this very private world but always groping in the dark? In reading
you I am half there and enjoying the upside down isles (like a map I
saw in Australia where it is on top of the world which <u>did</u> make me
slightly dizzy, and half I am lost between all those female epiphanies
but do not mind, because as M said "by leaving things out etc" – By
the way child(e) bairn, in dutch is kind, but I will resist the obvious
temptation.

[. . .] BBC wants to do something to/with *The Following Story*. (radio)
Well, I don't know, but at least something stirs in the isles, possibly
since you ? put them in their new position. [. . .]

All the best,

Cees

——

"Lisa's Story" and "On the 31st July" were first published as *Lisa Lisa: Two Prosays*
(2000); reprinted in *Poems &* (2012). Both pieces mention works by Noote-
boom, who first received pre-publication print outs. "Lisa's Story" includes a
parable of different approaches to crossing a river taken by a Hindu monk and
a Buddhist monk. *Lisa Lisa* includes a photo of "Wrest [*sic*] of Europe viewed
from space Copycat ABsat" showing, as related in "On the 31st July", that the
British Isles has indeed been turned upside down, during a solar eclipse.

——

[12]

Lewes   3 September 1999

Dear Cees
   No! I had no idea that it was your birthday 31st of July! That was
truly just the date that I sat down to begin to write that piece. I'm
mortified!
And yesterday a letter from AZ reminding me that <u>Pet</u> name resonates
with the childtalk of his regional dialect: Petèl!!! Too much . . . or not
enough . . . ?
Cees, I too have difficulties with all these old "broken" relationships
(and new ones perhaps not (yet) made). With <u>prose</u> I think I am always
still trying to find out <u>if</u> I can do it.
                        [. . .]
HAPPY BIRTHDAY (it's mine 10 Sept!)
                                            Anthony

                         ____

[Amsterdam]   [? May 2000]

Dear AB.   Forgive me this frivolous card which I found in Australia –
from which I have just come back. [. . .] Saw your letter in *Lettre* – I
wrote a piece (dutch) as a young columnist about the House of Lords
in the 60s. Of course it has to go, and yet, getting older, I tend to
become sentimental about those things. Will the world change when all
the crowns become plastic? The trouble with the last remnants of
mythology is that the roles have to be played by (mostly) decrepit
humans. On the other hand, I like dinosaurs – anyway I'm not rational
as you can see! [. . .] After three months absence I am facing a Pyrenean
landscape of mail – All the best and thank you for the new *Lisa!*   Cees

                         ____

Dear Cees!

The article in the paper you saw about H of L is not by me. It is by a political journalist with the same name with whom I have sometimes been confused (in public & in private – we have occasionally written in the same places) sometimes in quite funny ways. But I have won our little battle – from this year in the *Guardian/Observer* he has dropped the "h" so that he has become Antony instead of Anthony – so I guess he was quite disturbed by the confusion! I might tell you more about this later – it is really quite amusing. the best

Anthony

PS. *Unbuilt Netherlands* is a beautiful fascinating discovery – A.

PPS. Look in the book *Poetry of AB* top page 18 for more about the confusion!

———

It was a mistake to believe that the socio-political journalist Anthony Barnett had dropped his "h". He had not. Antony Barnett is a different socio-political journalist, who may, to avoid confusion, or may not, if it was not there in the first place, have dropped an "h". In *Unbuilt Netherlands* (Architectural Press, 1985) Nooteboom contributes an essay to visionary projects by Dutch architects—see AB, "Antonym: Fantastic, Fantastical" in *Tears in the Fence*, 60 (2014) for a discourse on this and a text by Andrea Zanzotto—see also letter fol.

———

[Amsterdam]   12.5.00.

Dear A·B·

Life is so much easier with initials! And also this: I have in my weird life written "political" pieces (as a columnist) – so I regard

these things as a natural extension though to find a poetic form for
them (as you so eloquently did in Ku Yuan) has never been my forte
when I see them back. Thanks for *Unbuilt* – there is now a new edition
in dutch/german elaborating a little bit on Benjamin and the flaneur.
The *Septentrion* essay goes to you not out of vanity but because you
are interested in translation. Next week off to Lisbon (poets) then as
soon as possible ± ½ June off to Summer Enclosure, where our cat
Vleermuis (Bat) will no longer, as the last 8 years, wait for us, because
she has desaparecido. Grief!   all the
            best   Cees

———

Ku Yuan: a poem entitled "©" combining a description of a poster by the artist
Ku Yuan, the fate of a copy, and the events of Tiananmen Square, written 5 June
1989. It was first printed as a card; then in *The Poetry of Anthony Barnett* (1993);
reprinted in *Poems &* (2012). *Septentrion*—see the two letters fol.

———

Lewes   18 June 2000

Dear Cees

    I wanted to tell you that a month ago I visited the *Lady & the Unicorn*
in Paris for the first time since I was a child. A neighbour of mine had
shown me your article on the tapestries in an English art journal. And
it made me look at them with fresh eyes. Thank you!
    Life is looking good: there is a new lady in my life [. . .]

                        Wishing you the very best
                        for the summer.

[15]

P.S. I lost my cat a few years ago too so I know that feeling.
PPS In your last card you mentioned an essay [. . .] ref. translation as if you were enclosing it, but there was nothing in the envelope apart from the card . . .

———

Life's Rich Tapestry: The Lady and the Unicorn appeared in *Art Quarterly* (Winter 1999).

———

San Luis   11.7.2^{000}.

Dear A B ,

Life must have more than two wings, it flies so quickly that I don't remember what I wrote you about translation, and what I forgot to enclose. Sorry.
Also I must have less than two eyes, since I cannot read what is new in your life. If it is not a lady it looks like a garden, but I doubt that you would give a hortus the same joyous emphasis. So it must be a lady and you have to keep your garden conclusus. Six (6!) tortoises seem to want to replace my cat.
I feed them the flowers that fall off the hibiscus every morning: they love it!   All the best,
                                  Cees

———

The seemingly missing essay was Françoise Opsomer, "Ses mots sont comptés: la poésie de Cees Nooteboom", trans. Isabelle Longuet, in *Septentrion: Arts, lettres et culture de Flandre et des Pays-Bas* (Rekkem, Belgique, décembre 1998), introducing a bilingual presentation by two translators of three poems. The issue was in fact never missing. It had been mailed under separate cover.

———

Amsterdam   26.10.2001

Dear Anthony,

       Thank you so much for these lovely books. Tarjei Vesaas
is really a great poet, and I would have never known him if not through
you. *All Saints Day* is coming out on the 9th November – and after an
initial complete lack of interest I have now to squeeze in a visit to
London Nov. 27 and 28, in between the U.S. and Florence. All far too
hectic – there will be a reception at the dutch embassy on Nov. 28 –
and though I know that you don't like that kind of thing I will ask
them to send you an invitation. The book looks strange, and to me
alienated from its content, but I have learned not to worry about those
things. It might be busy, with little time to talk, but maybe we can meet
up before or after. All best,
                                     Cees

just now received the "real" book – it looks better than I thought – so
you see . . .

Nooteboom writes *All Saints Day* in error for *All Souls' Day*. In fact, the true trans-
lated title of the Dutch original should simply be *All Souls* but the translation
of a novel with that title by Spanish author Javier Marías had been published
not long before, in 1999, so the decision was taken to publish Nooteboom's
novel under the slightly different title. AB attended the reception, which was
the second occasion on which he met Nooteboom and the first on which he
met Simone Sassen.

----

[17]

Pátzcuaro [Mexico]   7.12.06

Dear Anthony,

                    [...]

Well, we'll survive: from here I go to Campeche in Yucatan. And in
Germany – a different place – volume VIII of my collected w. have
appeared 880 pages. [vol. X in preparation as at 2014.] So not all is
lost! This whole letter was accompanied by loud Mexican music on this
most beautiful of plazas Plaza Quiroga in Pátzcuaro –

                         all best,
                           Cees

ps. My wife, Simone Sassen, and I have just published (Schirmer und
Mosel, Munich) a rather huge Photo book called TUMBAS ([title] in
Spanish): Graves of Poets and Philosophers in all the world, known
and less known – Proust is on the cover (his grave) – Auden in Austria,
Canetti, Joyce, Mann, Stevenson (in Samoa) Neruda (in Chile) Melville,
Gottfried Benn, etc. etc. No way it will be published in E or USA, but in
2008 in french, yes.

                         ——

                TUMBAS—see email, 29 April 2014.

                         ——

[Amsterdam] email   15 April 2014

        [...] *Snow* looks lovely so go ahead. Cees

                         ——

On receiving a proof for correcting, Nooteboom provided further elucidations in an email attachment. Some small items have been incorporated in the letter annotations. The remainder follow.

———

[Amsterdam] email attachment [edited]   29 April 2014

A curious detail: a recent duquesa de Medinaceli was known as the red duchess, la duquesa roja.

About the translation of *The Captain*: you will see David Comer's versions. The problem really is with *zicht, gezicht*. The latter really means *face*, a part of the book is called *Het Gezicht van het Oog*, and would then mean: *The Face of the Eye*, which is impossible, but *gezicht* can also mean *vision* – in the sense of a saint having a vision, and then also *fata morgana*. Then there are words like *vergezicht, perspective, prospect, vista, panorama*. Somebody can have *second sight, a view* is *een uitzicht, inzicht* can be as well *insight* as *opinion*. There is no end to it.

Also, for example, in the poem about Picasso, an engraving where an old man (P?) is secretly watching a couple make love – he then desires for himself one more *eeuwige* (*eternal*) *omgang*, which in dutch confessional terminology sometimes should be accompanied by *carnal: vleselijke omgang*. David has used *intercourse*, which is correct of course, but my french translator will use *commerce*, which I like a lot because of the double entendre.

By the way, it was my french publisher who took my detour away with an argument of (pseudo) cartesian clarity: "If a frenchman wants to go to Santiago de Compostela he goes directly, *pas de détours.*" The point of my book was of course just the opposite. The original title was and is *The Detour to Santiago*, german: *Der Umweg nach Santiago*.

[Adam] Thirlwell asked me to participate in a translation excercise which I did, translating a sort of student prank by a pseudonym of Kierkegaard from the english translation of a philosopher from the danish original – my translation then was translated back into english by Coetzee. [*Multiples: 12 Stories in 18 Languages by 61 Authors* (Portobello, 2013).] A much nicer idea was David Mitchell translating a piece by a japanese 19th century author, which then was translated into spanish by Valeria Luiselli, a brillant young mexican writer for whose book *Papeles Falsos* (*False Papers*, mistranslated into english as *Sidewalks*). For this Granta edition I wrote an essay as introduction (2013).

The Czech [16.1.99] was my friend Milos Sovac, prof. of medicine in the US, who, after he had escaped Czechoslovakia as a young officer in the back of a car, invented and patented important medicines, worked for a period in the Vatican printing office, learning all he could about paper, typography, etc., which he later used when he produced magnificent books for his Ettan Press, in Rancho Santa Fe, Cal.

If her (Virginia Woolf) ashes are where she died, our book TUMBAS (not in english) has a photograph Simone Sassen has made of the garden where the ashes were scattered. [Her, and her husband's, ashes were buried under elm trees. Virginia's came down in a hurricane; later, Leonard's succumbed to Dutch elm disease.] TUMBAS is a book of photographs (and texts) of poets and thinkers all over the world. V. W. has no grave, but the garden was beautiful. There is Wittgenstein's grave in Cambridge, Stevenson's in Samoa, Joyce in Zürich (near Canetti), Neruda on the Isla Negra in Chile, Proust, Beckett, Vallejo, Baudelaire, Susan Sontag in Paris, some of the graves like animistic altars. There are german, spanish, french and of course dutch versions of the book, death seems to frighten the anglo-saxons.

[Cees]

REI HAYAMA

The Focus

THE FOCUS
2013 / video / 25 min / Rei Hayama
Inspired by Nathaniel Hawthorne's story, "The Earth's Holocaust", the film was made
using photographs from a number of old books on natural history and ethnology.
Through their conversion across media, from paper to film, then to digital, the images
shed their original aura or distance from their subjects and merge into a story of a
village and its people. The texts inserted between the images are written in
both Japanese and English. The parallel sentences are connected across
the languages through literal translation and wordplay. The title
THE FOCUS connotes how meanings, once taken apart,
are reconstructed in the human mind.

TRAILER OF THE FOCUS

2013, video, black and white, 25 min

Inspired by Nathaniel Hawthorne's story, "The Earth's Holocaust", the film was made using photographs from a number of old books on natural history and ethnology. Through their conversion across media, from paper to film, then to digital, the images shed their original aura or distance from their subjects and merge into a story of a village and its people. The texts inserted between the images are written in both Japanese and English. The parallel sentences are connected across the languages through literal translation and wordplay. The title THE FOCUS connotes how meanings, once taken apart, are reconstructed in the human mind.

black

fog

THE WORLD

ONE DAY ある日

fog

INHABITANTS MADE A BONFIRE … は焼されてきた過去を 一掃するために、

… TO PURGE THEIR PRAISED PAST. 住民たちは、火を燃いた。

SHOULDERING RESPECTIVE PASTS, PEOPLE GATHER FROM DISTANT PLACES.

人々は、遠方から、各々の過去を背負って、集まる。

blue

bonfire

house1

house2

black

sleep! 眠りなさい!

black
house3

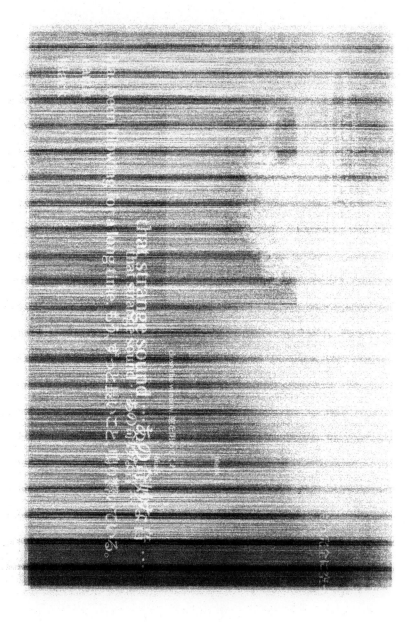

SUBTITLES TO THE FOCUS

00:00:00 black 黒

00:10:00 fog 霧

00:40:29 ONE DAY, ある日、

00:43:00 THE WORLD WAS BURIED IN A DARKNESS その世界は、闇に、埋もれた。

00:49:00 fog 霧

01:07:27 INHABITANTS MADE A BONFIRE … 賛美されてきた過去を　一掃するために、

01:12:17 … TO PURGE THEIR PRAISED PAST. 住民たちは、火を焚いた。

01:18:02 bonfire blue 焚火青

01:48:23 bonfire red 焚火赤

02:15:28 blue 青

02:24:13 nebula 星雲

02:42:03 SHOULDERING RESPECTIVE PASTS, PEOPLE GATHER FROM DISTANT PLACES.
人々は、遠方から、各々の過去を背負って、集まる。

02:53:20 house1 家1

03:05:22 house2 家2

03:17:16 black 黒

03:29:08 sleep! 眠りなさい!

03:32:12 black 黒

03:43:02 house3 家3

03:57:09 if you leave the window open all night, お前が、一晩中、窓を開け放ったままでいるならば

04:05:22 black 黒

04:07:20 i'm going insane. わたしは、気が狂うだろう。

04:12:07 black 黒

04:24:12 people left. 人々は、去っていった。

04:28:12 it seems this town became completely empty now … 街は、もう完全に空っぽね …

04:35:15 black 黒

04:44:11 close the window. 窓を閉めてくれ。

04:50:25 black 黒

04:53:13 that strange sound … あの奇妙な音 …

04:57:13 black 黒

04:58:17 has been blowing for a long time. もう、ずっと長いこと、鳴り響いている。

05:03:26 earth 大地

05:31:11 black 黒

[continue]

[26]

ANTHONY BARNETT

A Sake Cup [1]

Usually, in fact up till now not at all, I do not publish what I call my Antonyms in a review of which I am an editor. These so-called Antonyms first appeared, the first six, in a journal of the English Association *The Use of English*. When its then editor, known to readers of *Snow*, departed he took on the role of reviews editor at *Tears in the Fence*. My Antonyms followed. With one exception, "The Publisher", that is where they have been appearing ever since. I write them for nothing—I wish it were otherwise because writing should be paid for even if it isn't—because I am allowed to write whatever I wish, without editorial meddling in such matters as punctuation. This is not trivial. It is important. Anyway, this sake cup of mine is a different kettle of fish, a different cup of sake, altogether. It might be that it should not be called an Antonym at all because I think it is a wholly positive piece, free of oppositional contradictions.

✳

"Form"—"It was an iron sake flask. There was a moment when this thread pattern flask taught him the beauty of 'form'." These beautiful lines make a complete section of *A Fool's Life* by Akutagawa Ryūnosuke. [2] The Japanese word for this thread pattern is itome. It might be that the translation should simply read "itome flask". I would like to think that I have experienced a similar, quiet eureka moment.

This happened while I was staying with my companion, without whose help I could not have translated *A Fool's Life*, in a beautiful traditional house a stone's throw from the sea a short wintery pine-clad hill drive from Kanazawa on the Noto Peninsular. One day we took a bus and a local train that ran beside water meadows with herons to meet a friend in nearby Wajima, a city famous for inventing a unique method of lacquerware production, Wajima-nuri, in the Ishikawa Prefecture of the snowy Hokuriku region. But this is not about lacquerware.

Strolling in Wajima's daily Morning Market, a low-roofed street filled with stalls and stores of all kinds, we entered a small pottery shop, doors open wide on to the street. The shelves displayed sake flasks and cups and other ware, greyish, metal-looking, which I picked up and put down, examining them in a sheepish effort to look for all the world as if I knew what I was doing, before I decided to settle on the one I wanted to buy.

This most modest unostentatious cup came with a paper slip, I have managed not to lose it, explaining the history and characteristics of this ware, which my companion has translated. Here it is adapted.

*

History recounts that a variety of pottery was in production for four hundred years, beginning in the Heian period, around the tenth to eleventh centuries, lasting into the Muromachi period, around the fourteenth century, in a small village named Suzu, located at the north-eastern most tip of the Noto Peninsula. This pottery was used for everyday ware over quite a large area, to the north of, and to the far north of, the Kansai region, centred in Kyoto. The pottery was produced in large quantities and transported as far as Hokkaidō by the famous convoy ships bearing the name Kitamaebune, which followed the route along the Sea of Japan. Suddenly, during the Sengoku period, the age of Japan's civil wars, around 1400–1600, the pottery disappeared and came to be known as ancient phantom or rare pottery ware.

In the mid 1950s the kiln remains at Suzu were excavated, to widespread attention. Archeologists and historical researchers named the pottery Suzu-yaki, Suzu ware. In Shōwa 53, 1978, after the long sleep of four hundred years, the restored kiln at Suzu was relit for firing. Since then, the number of Suzu kiln houses and masters of the special skills required has steadily increased. It is curious that four hundred years of production was followed by four hundred years of sleep.

*

Suzu ware is characterized by a simplicity, taken over from the skills found in Japanese Sue pottery, brought to Japan from the Continent, the Korean Peninsula, by Korean potters in the mid Tumulus period, around the fifth century. It uses the soil around Suzu, containing a high proportion of iron, to which a very high temperature is applied, more than 1200° celsius. The pottery is unglazed in a method called kusube-yaki, smoked out. The iron in the soil, combining with the carbon, produces a somber beauty of grey-black colour. The ash from the burnt logs works to cover the pottery in a natural glaze of delicate tones known as hai-katsugi, ash-covered. Over the years, the more regularly it is used, this yaki jime sekki, pottery fired fiercely at high temperature, takes on a most harmonious texture. It is best not to hide it away in a cupboard but to keep it out on the cup board with the sake.

*

I handed the cup I wanted to buy to the shopkeeper, I think he was wearing spectacles, who turned it in his hand, smiling approvingly, saying "You have made a very good choice." Like the modest earthenware holy grail in that film. Well, I have to admit that I felt rather pleased with myself, even if that is not as modest.[3]

---

[1] The end e in all Japanese words, sake, itome, Sue, etc, is sounded as é.
[2] Akutagawa Ryūnosuke, *A Fool's Life*, trans. Anthony Barnett and Toraiwa Naoko (Lewes, Allardyce Book, 2007), repr. with corrections in Anthony Barnett, *Translations* (Lewes, Tears in the Fence, in assoc. Allardyce Book ABP, 2012).
[3] The cup is shown on page 192.

JASON KAO HWANG

SYMPHONY OF SOULS

Recorded by Jason Kao Hwang and Spontaneous River
24 April 2010, Systems Two, Brooklyn, NY
Released 2011 CD Mulatta MUT022
Video of the complete session posted at
www.youtube.com/watch?v=iKch6kft2ZY

Spontaneous River, based in New York City, is an orchestra of thirty-seven string im-
provisers plus drum set. In recent years more and more string players have engaged in
the art of improvisational music in large ensembles. Spontaneous River is an ensemble
and a community that represents this growing movement. The power of Spontaneous
River is drawn from both the sonic unity of strings and the undeniable individualism
of each musician's "voice". *Symphony of Souls* is a spontaneous flow of notated passages
and conducted improvisations that sing stories of life journey through abundant sound
emanating from blues, jazz, classical and world sources. Thomas Stanley writes in the
liner notes to the released recording: "The orchestra is then summoned to explore soul
as both a nexus of dialog and as the motive force compelling action and interaction. 'I
felt in this one unified sound, I could hear the voice of each soul,' Jason recalls, 'The
music was a whole tree, but you could hear each individual leaf in motion.'"   JKH

COMPOSER, CONDUCTOR, VIOLIN: Jason Kao Hwang
DRUM SET: Andrew Drury
VIOLIN: Trina Basu, Sarah Bernstein, Charles Burnham, Julianne Carney
Mark Chung, Fung Chern Hwei, Rosi Hertlein, Elektra Kurtis, Gwen Laster
Marlene Rice, Dave Soldier, Curtis Stewart, Midori Yamamoto, Helen Yee
VIOLA: Leanne Darling, Nicole Federici, Judith Insell, Eric Salazar, David Wallace
GUITAR: Cristian Amigo, Bradley Farberman, James Keepnews, Dom Minasi
David Ross, Tor Snyder, Hans Tammen
CELLO: Martha Colby, Loren Dempster, Daniel Levin, Tomas Ulrich, Shanda Wooley
STRING BASS: Michael Bisio, Ken Filiano, Francois Grillot, James Ilgenfritz
Clifton Jackson, Tom Zlabinger

Symphony of Souls is created through orchestral improvisation that is conducted by a lexicon of hand gestures (see below) in dialogue with sixteen written passages. Generally the score progresses left to right, with earlier sections reappearing in variations, often with cued fermatas and transpositions. The conductor can cue the whole orchestra or sections or individuals to perform written passages. The conductor indicates passages 1 through 5 with the five digits on one hand. Ear 1 through 5 is indicated by the left hand holding the left ear, and digits 1 through 5 of the right hand. Heart 1 through 5 is indicated by the right hand over the heart, with digits 1 through 5 of the left hand. "Arm Up to the Sky" is cued as described. "Waving 5" (measure 25), is cued by waving five digits of one hand. "Top" is indicated with the hand on top of the head. Cues 2, 3, Ear 1, Ear 2, Ear 3 and Heart 3 can be cued in time or with note-to-note fermatas. They can also be transposed as cued by the conductor.

LEXICON OF CONDUCTED IMPROVISATIONAL CUES

TRADITIONAL
• downbeat (traditional)
• held note (open palm)
• cut-off

PITCH
• sustained fermata – note to note
    – assigning leaders to cue sustained notes
• sustained followed by slides – RH downbeat, LH curve down, RH cut
• high notes – point up
• low notes – point down
• drone on D – arc both arms over head

TRANSPOSITION
• ½ step – from nose up to top of head
• whole step up – chin up to top of head
• whole step – chin up to top of head
• minor third – chin to above head
• fourth – chest to way above head

- pianissimo, forte – shhh and fist
- cresc, decresc – v up and down
- mute – cover

TEXTURE
- tremelo – mime bow trememlo
- bird calls (above finger board) shake hand above head
- pizz – mimed
- harmonics – hand circle (ok)
- crunch – mime
- mime: guitar tight – squeeze to chest; strings mime bow crunch
- colegno – mimed colegno
- wide vibrato – mimed
- trill – flat palm rotated rapidly back and forth
- gliss – follow shape of hand gesture
- air sounds – shhh (strings blow across f holes)
- tremelo / flutter tongue – bow tremelo
- pitch bends – gesture down or up
- wide vibrato
- drunk improv – rubbery stretches

DRUM SET
- arco cymbals or slides on drum

MUTES
- mute (*cover bridge for strings*)

DOUBLE-STOPS (strings) / MULTIPHONICS (reeds)
- interlaced fingers

IMPROVISATION
- solos – point and come hither gesture
- call & response – each hand gestures talking
- short stabs – tiger claw
- guitars comp – mime strum
- repeat or riff – hands bracket
- improv – solo or sectional – come hither!

- call & response – talking bird
- open more space – hands pulled apart
- develop – hand circles encouragement
- break up pattern
- arpeggio – follow shape of hand gesture
- riffs cues from conductor's violin
- improv runs up or down – use arm, trace finger up or down
- conducted rhythms – follow gestured rhythm
- conduct any written cue as note to note fermatas

ASSIGN LEADERS
- create riff – point to leader, eye to ear, riff gesture
- create sustained, point to leader, eye to ear, sustain

GROOVES
- ostinato 4/4
- walk 4/4
- shuffle 4/4 (digging triplet gesture)
- 6/8 conducted
- break groove and develop
- guitar comp (mime strum)

CONDUCTOR GENERATED
- cues from my violin
- conducted rhythms

Combination example
- forte piano (fist + shh)
- accent / trill / gliss (fist – hand flutter – slide)

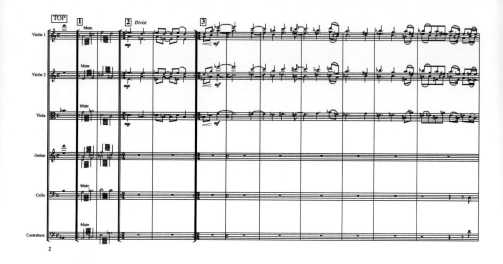

WAVING
5

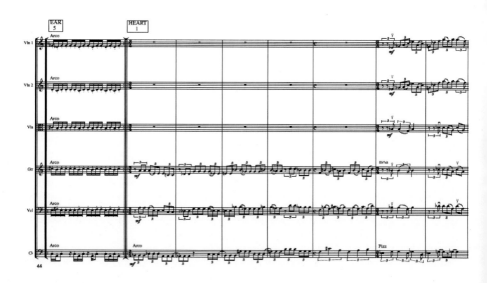

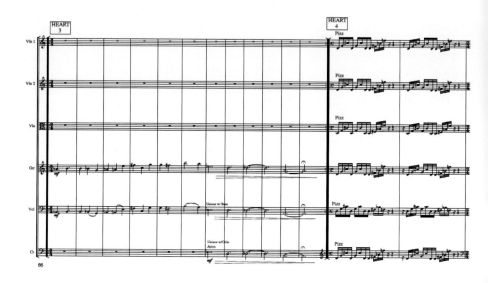

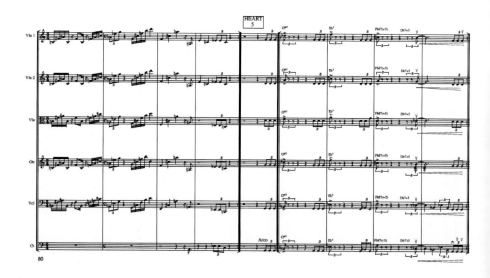

ANDREA ZANZOTTO

translated from the Italian by

CHRISTINA CHALMERS &
CONCETTA SCOZZARO

Infancies, Poetries, Nursery
(notes)

1. Poetry and infancy? Yes, perhaps it's worth the pain of returning to a tired cliché, if it's true that clichés often have roots in profundity, carrying an echo of it, and sometimes much more than that. We are talking about two realities between which it is often too easy to recognise a special relation. It is probably in the inevitable fact that they tend to appear to be complicated by mythic and symbolic tensions when we seek to bring them together (bring them back together)—to understand them from the inside, as lived—that the most compelling reason exists to admit the necessity of this relation. And this is still the case even if today we are certainly not lacking attempts to see clearly into the question, accepting as well as overcoming presuppositions of this kind.[1]

It's a fact, however, that especially in our time, from halfway through the last century onwards, the idea and practice of poetry have in a very particular way sharpened their focus on childhood, returning to and scrutinising certain themes of Rousseauian and romantic origin. Poetry has always been identified with a desire to return to the child's world or with a regret for what has been lost or even with a childish manner.[2] But at the same time, the conventional and quite unreal idea we used to have of the child came to change so that infancy on the one hand continued to represent the time of the highest emotional and fantastical richness of humanity, but on the other hand, lost many of its idyllic attributes, assuming more and more a figure within the drama of originary and antagonistic forces of the psyche and the environment, creating irreversible conditions that are destined to determine the life of every single individual. In certain areas, even the human sciences seem to confirm the ancient intuition of an intimate connectivity between childhood and poetry for better or for worse (if we can put it like that): from cultural anthropology and psychoanalysis, from prehistoric science and from linguistics, thinkers came to realisations that could have also meant a clarification of the connivance between these two worlds with their blurred boundaries, but were reluctant to make definitions that were too certain; instead (especially in terms of poetry) their research became more and more specialised. Poetry and infancy, following new stimuli, discoveries and recognitions, seemed to be attached to the inside of a metaphoric scheme in which each of the two terms was able to symbolise the other, even if in an accidental and uneasy relation, based on analogies that were sometimes flimsy and sometimes dazzling, that could take form on the most diverse levels.

We can look for example at what multiplicity of implications it is that comes to assume the characterisation as poetry, in relation to infancy-awakening, even if it is emphasized only in the aspects of its mnemonic validity; though we must take care to remember to recognise the primacy of memory (in the whole arc of its meanings and resonances) both in terms of the foundation of the cultural structures of various ethnic groups and in individual psychic structures. The chains of rhythms and sounds along which tradition was transmitted and made available: these were born directly from the physicality of man, from his same biological rhythms, framed inside those of the world that created them: "cosmic", then, in a certain sense. Research carried out for decades, that today probably finds its most active synthesis in the work of Leroi-Gourhan, attests that memory created a common cultural store for social groups in formation—gestures and words, techniques and myths, notions and passions—drawing laws of permanence and of transmission from those laws of global psycho-physical homogeneity, in all its living rhythms. Even with this universal human behaviour in mind, with its capacities for cultural foundation, we cannot deny that poetry—which is evidently preserved and strengthened in the flourishing of the popular and the epic that accompanies the beginning of history and almost marks it—is most tenacious in resisting, in also reappearing later.

Analogously, the babbling of early childhood—sounds which are still inarticulate but loaded with expressive powers, melody that in some way is already significant, born from a complex of muscular activity tending to harmony—is the root of creative speech, conjoined to the same possibility of memory. The primary structuring of psychic "continuity", of memory-identity, in which the dynamic of originary fantasies comes to dwell, is accomplished even in the varied game made with these phonic elements and their laws: from the gentle canto of baby-talk and from interjective sounds to the very first syllables of children (which are not just by chance iterative) and then to words, to the singing of nursery rhymes, or the rhythmic series in which language is proposed and accepted as whimsical self-production, *autopoesis*. In these beginnings the enchanted web of signifiers already appears released into its own space, in which the already unforeseeable and mysterious world of things—referents—seems to be carried into the unforeseeable and the unthinkable. Continuity and identity are also fluency, fluid rhythm; memory, capable of recognition, is also fantasy; the necessary psycho-physical drives redefine themselves in *ludus liberatore*. And in this way (one of the most decisive) play enters into the scene, an essential element for primary formation even in animals, producing an experience of magic under the feeling of a power obtained over persons and things thanks to the use of names and later in their risky (yet still "playful") systemisation into phrases.

Infancy grows in time like this, new words peep out between these notes, seducing more than disconcerting or repulsing. Maternal voice, voices of the atmosphere, voice-colours, figures and images of the world and of the emerging Is remain fused in an impalpable unity, at the depths resolved in the apparitions of poetry-language. The child laughs in a fall-surprise at the falling cadence which is kidnapped away through two final sections of verse; the child is subtly alarmed by the infinite repetition ("É la storia del sor Vincenzo / che la dura tanto tempo / e che mai no la se destriga: / vustu che te la conta o vustu che te la diga?");* he is induced to sleep by the "cradle songs" in which a type of "hypnotic-stupefying" function of language, on the brink of dissolving itself into sounds, and at the limit of the conative function, joins in happy journeying wake sleepwake sleep dreams (nothing). Knowledge of things and their names occurs in this atmosphere loaded with affectivity and with phonic-rhythmic inventions; the story of the appropriation of names, a process of denotation always complicated by connotative facts, is consubstantial to the story of each individual and to the story of the figure that the world comes to assume for every symbol. And this while the traditions of oral folklore, a lineage more viscerally true and more popular in the collective, is utilised from the very beginning in all its possibilities. Certain exemplary pages from Michel Leiris are direct documents that carry back a living experience of such processes, the events of this "production of the self"; it is also important to remember, in this and adjacent fields, the fundamental acquisitions of the schools of psychology, of various orientations (from Piaget to Klein to Lacan) or the recognitions of the linguists (from Jakobson to Fonagy to Valesio). There is much to say on the relation between "the essence of poetry" and this initial phase in which language cannot but be egocentric, narcissistic, in which echolalia serves that which is effectively a monologue (even in the form of collective monologue when children find themselves brought together), and in which reality becomes invested by an imaginative activity moving always towards the desirable, according to the "pleasure principle".

In the progressive development of the psyche, in the various stages of infancy up to the threshold of adolescence, while language opens out to its fully social nature, the practical and logical capacities, as well as

* Veneto dialect—trans.

every other form of supplemental power, install themselves against that background and continue in part to live from it, even if they are specified as being authentic, independent facts. But, as proved in experiment,[3] for most of their childhood children show that they prefer expression substantiated by rhythm and sound: the same tale versified (and sung) is much more pleasurable than its "version in prose"; in the meantime, the capacity to pick up poetic discourse at a high level begins to manifest itself. Even the force of figurative expression of the poetic image begins to be picked up very early, returned to stupefying variations, relived *ex novo*; the drawings of children as "comments" to poems offer ample documentation of this, generating an equally imposing series of scientific investigations in that direction in our period.

But, unexpectedly, that progressive impoverishment and frustration of creativity occurs,[4] in which the atmosphere (especially the precocious aggressions of the media) and the aberrant structures of society have some part, but which has especially to do with the school-nursery, which often massacres even with the most tender and saintly intentions. Poetry-language-memory declines stingy straining towards a wholly exterior mnemo-technics, finalised in a fragmentary and heterogeneous didacticism; the paraphrase which destroys texts in a grotesque grammatological bricolage, in scarred anatomic specks, arrives, emphasised above all other knowledge. And here then the imposition of "poetry by heart" is not the affective and completely free choice of a poem or collection (it doesn't matter) to learn "par coeur": with the result that one either hates poetry forever or at the most that poetry serves us with materials for gratifying and vacuous citations, which the professional—with his "humanistic culture"—believes add sugar to his little phrases. This doesn't always happen, another discourse is also often tried in school; but what results do we see altogether?

Poetry then—or at least one of its immediate modes of appearance—remains at the root of the human world, both in phylogenetics and in cultural ontogeny, if we can speak of it as such. This also occurs for the simple fact that in the poetic function of language, taking "joy" and "conscience" in one's own existence gives back all of that existence's history, reassumes all its potentials, reactivates or re-presents in a nutshell all the other of its functions and finally, if you will, expresses its nature as a structural foundation of humanity. At this point the problem of the arrangement and sense that poetry must have—as verses (but also not), in the global educative process and in school-nursery—manifests its intimative implications, its conditioning nature: this even if poetry had to be dissolved, as today there is reason to fear it will be, in aporias (similar to those that threaten the pedagogic act). They are aporias that we nonetheless might find lead us back to the necessity of an overcoming, because they are in fact "unpronounceable".

2. In our time, when the historic social and cultural crisis entered an unprecedented climax, the consonances between poetry and childhood could not but come to be investigated (fantasised) with feverish insistence, in complex, ambiguous and even contradictory forms. If Decadence was in certain respects the revelation of the obliteration of the integral human figure, almost so that—for the impossibility of bearing the antinomies in which reason seemed destined to lose itself—it was necessary to give up "maturing" in order to survive; all the forms of humanity, or even of pre-humanity, "arrested" at the dawn, became a point of reference and at the same time a refuge. In a climate of the "destruction of reason" (it is right, but not completely sufficient, to return to Lukàcsian reflections) adolescence, infancy (and wildness at its limit) were the realities which one found oneself thrown behind, with greater or lesser satisfaction. But this retreat paradoxically involved the acquisition of new modes of approaching childhood and adolescence, an authentic awareness of their effective problems, a new capacity to re-experiment these problems from the intimate outwards, even if this remained between inevitable "illegitimate" mythologisations and the dangers of "improper use". The child passed therefore into the foreground, it became a term of comparison, a kind of a model.

[45]

All of this was verified concomitantly with the development of various pedagogies of activism (with masters of yet very different ideological roots, from Decroly to Montessori right up to Ferrière and Dewey) which offered new bases, scientific ones as well, for that type of action which had always been in the programmes of true pedagogy: which poses the child as a subject and not as an object of the educative act. But we must underline exactly an ambiguity in the whole complex of the situation: infancy exalted as a regressive refuge on one side, infancy as subject of revolution on the other side; infancy as a symbol tending to universal comprehensiveness, yet always more central (especially in literature) as an irrationalistic symbol; and infancy stripped bare scientifically, outside every idealisation, understood to be the seat of innocence but also of "polymorphous perversity", a stupendous eruption of life as well as a moment which founds irreversibility (as in Freudian research).

It is true moreover that the theme of the mysterious primacy of infancy had been a permanent theme in Western culture, and not only Western; well-noted are its incarnations: from the child gods of religion and the ancient poems to the little boy-Platonic poet, from the *puer* that comes from the sky to install a new order to the *pueri* who necessarily address the singing of poetry, to the *parvuli* one must resemble in order to enter the kingdom of heaven. We are not lacking the cunning variant of the theme: from the new-born God who is already a petty thief such as Mercury to the boy rogue such as Lazarillo. In fact, however, these had always been emblems of a counterculture; the same "true" pedagogy, aiming to dispel the master, was always counterculture. The heavy hand, the arrogance of the father-master had always prevailed; similarly, poetry did not in fact consider children except casually, nor did there exist a poetry particularly directed at children. Partial instrumentalisation of the tale "with a moral at the end", didacticism in forced and ungraceful, pseudo-rhythmical moulds; these were as much as one was able to propose to infancy as "its" poetry through most of the West: but this was already something more than the mere void, or almost, of the preceding centuries.

Coming from the "green paradises" of "infantile loves" to pass on ahead, finally, the *puer*: angel and a little bit devil too, in a time at the end of times, a time of the aeon's flux. Certainly this infant had to do above all with Rimbaud, the "poet of seven years", who even finished by pronouncing a curse against poetry which prefigures (and exhausts)—in the child and adolescent overwhelmed by silence—poetry as revolution-auto-combustion of infancy, to which the adult and adultism cannot be the successive moment, even less the negation. But with this *puer* Pascoli also had to do, who, in Maria Pascoli's testimony, wrote a prayer in Latin underneath the image of the Madonna and her little one, in which he invoked from the holy child the capacity to teach, like he did, pure songs to children: almost in an obscure and ardent delirium of "religion of infancy-poetry". A none less magic return to the child self—tormented by illness—did R. L. Stevenson accomplish, expert of every "duplicity" and adventure of the fantastic, with his 1885 *A Child's Garden of Verses*, turning towards children in a new way.

Since the end of the last century, we have seen the formation of a new tradition in which encounters between poetry and infancy alternately take priority over one another, creating sensational effects in various fields of culture, with much new material emerging thanks to such encounters, which have become respected for their authenticity.

3. In this atmosphere, tendencies towards the creation of a poetry centred on childhood (on "possible infancies") tangled together until they were almost completely confused; along with those tendencies that turned back to give to the child a poetry that was finally more suited to him, producing along specialist lines or making a better choice between the "common" elements; while one was brought increasingly to consider the expression of children as poetry.

The first situation created a true and proper gallery of myths, all of them more or less valid in their disquieting splendour, in a series of mimetic or pseudo-mimetic attempts to produce an encounter with infancy, sometimes resulting in a new legibility for children and often with the effective re-conquest of their world, as was said then. The second situation is connected in large part with the poetics of the preceding, but used in a rather more extrinsic and intellectualistic form, and inevitably posing as epigonism, even if, in some rare cases, quite contentedly. A renewal, at least, occurred, of the epigonism of the didactic kind of childhood poems, which predominated in the nineteenth century; metric and stylistic schemes of the late-Romantic type came to be abandoned—and, even, the eighteenth-century fable was rising again.

The "will" to speak of the child in his own language, to understand him and respect his specificity, had to in any case give origin—exactly because of an excess of "intention"—to a poetic production not only of dubious value, but also uncertain as regards functionality. In fact, apart from that, in the Crocean line, it remains always correct to doubt the characterisation of something as poetry "from the outside" (here, on the basis of precise demands of the addressee); there still remain in play the equivocal products precisely of the (good) will of the authors and of the phantasms that drove that will forward: first among these, the idea or the more or less distorted feeling of one's "own" infancy, implied as a perspectival point in speaking to children, or again the certainty of one's own "full" even if "very humble" and "confidential" maturity. Wishful thinking, banalities, clumsiness, caricature were, therefore, all destined to align easily with the works born from these programmes.

As for the third case, an advantage was realised in one major respect, if not in any others: a greater attention towards the child's spontaneous productions, which are often incredibly rich with imaginative fecundity and with an expressive impulse to enter into poetry, an impulse which is beyond any inscription of "artistic intent". Cases of child poets are often not very significant (this can also be emphasised artificially, like those quite recent examples of Minou Drouet or Antonio Fortichiari or Giovanni Serafini, even if these poets are not negligible); but "poems" written by children really exist, they form themselves where school consents to an actually free use of language, oral and written, and they have much to teach us all in the invincible, fine, crude truths that they carry, further than the fact of their rhythmic value and their fantasy.[5] The same happens elsewhere in the graphic works of children, even if today people tend to value them more than seems appropriate within the limits of their function as psychograms.

Further, at the margins, we must also remember the apparition of a barely visible thread of poetry which draws on pedagogical issues more or less linked to practices within the nursery, seen not solely through the eyes of the child, but also through the eyes of teachers, caught between a depressing everyday life and the troubles of theorising and research. It is a line that in certain respects parallels the lineage that in prose work has had a much larger acknowledgement, above all with the emphasis on the grotesque, by Gombrowicz and Mastronardi, to mention a few significant names.

As such, the presence of childhood in our modern culture, born from a social remorse, from a will to flight or from the enthusiasm of a discovery, remains productive and characteristic even in its obsessiveness. Literature in prose and poetry—in the most secret depths of its fashion ing—are affected dramatically by this presence. We should also remember, for example, Lewis Carroll, perhaps singular in global significance and widely-held esteem, the prestigious father who galvanised poetry with prose and logic (mathematics) towards a common goal of childhood found behind the mirror, of "rebirth", of "transfiguration", for a childhood that proposes liberty from every known schema and reinvents the world for everyone.

4. In terms of the interaction between the above-mentioned different levels (and the game of suggestiveness between convergent cultural sectors) we might be interested to give a brief glance at how much this has come about in our poetry, without entering into foreign creative production, especially since this would pose, in relation to our pedagogical

reflections, the problem of translation. This is different in different cases, depending on whether it concerns "authors" *tout court*, even if understood as childhood reading, like Rilke and Lorca, or instead of poets that are more than anything else "specialists" such as the truly virtuosic Marshak, or of the productions of popular poetry, especially of the Third World— finally less neglected than in the past. But a recognition of the Italian situation, though still limited because of the now almost pan-global character of many of the phenomena which that literature displays, can equally be revelatory.

Here, again, we start from the true child-monster that Pascoli is, that Zvanì is, "divinely" dead, embroiled in the labyrinth of his complexes, blocked by the censure against eros at the thresholds of adolescence in a climate of white incest. One might overlook the authentic Pascolian puerility even in its most excessive moments: Pascoli in half-light in the halo-womb of the family of origin, lost in the infinite pursuit of rhythmic-phonic games, in the capillary titillation of a thousand sensations as spiked with concretion as doubled with phantasmatic and symbolic folds. He uses the force of an adult in the service of the infantile chrysalis, in fable grown to its full proportions without ever developing itself. And existing in such an amputated state, dimensions are revealed to him of lost countries, treasures, objects and encounters, parental figures and figures from the atmosphere of infancy but also of "another" infancy, a mode of being that will never be given a fitting name.

The Twilight Poets call themselves little boys and sometimes they are almost that in reality, like Corazzini. Their discourse never fails to refer to bittersweet boyhood, they wander in half-enclosed gardens in a world to which we must return to save ourselves, for a moment at least, even if perhaps we have never left it at all, or if perhaps instead we have lost the entrance. From Moretti to Gozzano to A. S. Novaro to Betti to Valeri (whose works, standing out for their warm affability and "discharged" but extremely fine elegance, have been rightly felt to be exemplary), several authors of this group or those around it naturally find the right path

towards a certain type of infantile interlocutor, in a climate of shared ten-
derness, of nostalgia and of a sensitivity-sensuality which gives a sharp
phonic body to their parts, open to the impromptu fresh and coloured
trouvailles and to the memory of popular cadences. But it is not a coinci-
dence that the specialist epigonism stood in large part on the basis of
these same positions, which came to be imagined as comfortable. We
are talking of a legion from which a Pezzani, a Dell'Era, a Schwarz or a
Fanciulli (as well as several other authors) are just emerging: people who
follow these patterns, always more and more fatigued, until they reach
the verge of the 1970s, often revealing a total absence of consciousness
of the problems of their own practice.

In the environs of the experimentalism of the Futurists, Palazzeschi
presents himself as interpreter of another idea-modality of infancy, a
little *enfant terrible*, who is capable of making jokes which go beyond the
"innocent" game and who knows mild poisons. Candid and sly, between
chipped signifiers and signifieds, between delightful sing-songs that are
perhaps even parodies, with his child-like-archetypal treatment à la Klee
(one thinks of the tempting example *Rio Bo*), Palazzeschi touches on
regression with the exquisite irresponsibility which accompanies him
("leave me alone so I can have fun!"), considering all his different dis-
tances from regression, flighty man and child of smoke. Folgore, Gov-
oni and others remain in those scenes, between illusionisms, chromatic
sizzles and pseudo-judgements; and here certain sympathetic specialist
followers come to be found, unassuming, such as Sergio Tofano or the
less convincing Vamba.

In the inter-war years, and with the arrival of the existential-hermetic
era (which marks the consciousness of a more profound break) there
appears also a new necessity, in defence of the anguished overflowing
of the sense of nothingness: the necessity for a totalising *gnosis* and for
the confrontation with a new responsibility: but as prison sentence, be-
cause what remains is the sense of impossibility, radicalised. Sbarbaro the
"whimsical child" had sensed all of this, in his feeling himself constrained

to an adultism without escape even in resignation, in a relation with the father which presents analogies to the Kafkaesque relation to the father.[6] Ungaretti speaks of poetry as the unquenched hope of childhood in an essay of the extraordinarily significant title "Innocence and Memory"; his strategy is to "Enjoy / one sole minute / of the first life" (in *Girovago*), but more and more clearly poetry delineates itself to him as "the life of a man" in its whole arc. Montale, "aged child", sees the paper boats from afar or in a kind of already incomprehensible close-up; he is in the "end of childhood"; life presents itself to him almost in a dichotomy of infancy/old age, to which ultimate end adult life cannot not resolve itself immediately. But the first term—infancy—is part of the most precious glimmers of the "life which glimmers"; and in *Satura* the rank of "tender and ferocious" children-elves appears, without "love of God and opinions", inexplicable like life itself, less than ever amenable to a meaning, arrested in front of the ellipsis of a finale (*Un mese tra i bambini*).

However, Ungaretti, who as soon as out of the grip of denial restores the primary movements of language-poetry—a primeval necessity and purity of words and of minimal syntactic links, of rhythms biologically nourished once more—approaches the territories of infancy along his own paths, especially in *Allegria*, so that his naked phrase "vie initiale" is easily received and appropriated by the child. And always when the discourse of the hermetics (as in Quasimodo, where it is more Sicilian-Greek, closer to the myth of origins) becomes elementary, the nascent language of a lost paradise which is for an instant recaptured, it comes to be transposed by the child, even in moments of maximal analogic tension, in its essence as music of syntactic elements and of concepts, not solely of sounds. The reductive and healing operations performed on language are made, creating the sense of a recovery of memory-primordium in a space of lucidity, typical of this poetic vein, so that infancy (especially in its twilight) succeeds in appreciating more than it seems to (as the practice of teaching demonstrates). Surrounding the vague "Ungarettism" and "Quasimodoism", a certain nineteenth-century free-verse-istic *koine* coagulates, pressing them into a pseudo-facility-(spontaneity) which also includes poetic experiences that have just passed: even within the scope of this *koine*, the messing around that "producers" for children are involved in has found means of being practiced.

Apart from the others there is the "little Berto", Saba, who so tempestuously knew how to seize creative possibilities in the encounter between psychoanalysis and poetry. In Saba crepuscular survivals are complicated by restless lights until they welcome Freudian remnants; from psychoanalysis he takes especially the established infancy themes,[2] and he continually revisits the period which runs from early childhood to adolescence (including all the iridescent and multiplying substrates); he asks to see the fruits of the investigation, realised in the conscious attempt to descend into his own profound beginnings, thanks to psychotherapy. Between this humanity of the child and then of the young man (always crudely enigmatic figures even in their fascination), Saba recovers the choral humanity of the city (remember the personification of Trieste in an adolescent), he recovers the world of those games such as football in which the common soul and the child's soul are reunited; he reconquers daily life and at the same time opens up discussions of the civil-social. The harmony of Saba's verse, which would like to be "natural" and seductive in its beautiful inheritance of tradition, is instead complex and involved in a contrast which, if on one hand brings the poet closer to the coveted freshness of the sensuous world, on the other hand inclines him towards an almost mystifying use of convention. But when he enters into absolute levity, channelling judgment and experience into you, he signals another possible path for a poetry indebted to childhood, along which other poets arrive, such as Penna, with his figurines of innocence at its limits, or Caproni with his seaside cities, animated by family gods. And then Sinisgalli, Sereni.

Surrealist literary research was developed in France, with the valorisation of automatic writing (even though, perhaps, this automatism did not succeed in truly involving the most subterranean stratas of the in-

[53]

dividual and collective psyche); it had revived a type of "free" discourse, of "poésie ininterrompue", where trends reappeared: sing-song, litany and reiterated strophic renewals—used in a sweet-obsessive way. Breton, Desnos pushed to extreme ends, Eluard with his more effulgent inventive expansion, Prévert at the heights of popular inspiration; all these gave back honours to the originary aspects of the poetic "word". Against a background of Freud and Marx, or at least an idea of revolution, they were rallied to justify this. This line is comparable to the Anglo-American current which goes from nonsense (Lear) and from the limerick to the nursery rhyme; and again, the presence of Carroll in such an area must be recognised almost as a junction and pre-emption: according to what was to be the aspiration of the Surrealists, the paradoxes of reality and language come to be discovered by the gaze of Alice, through the point of view of mad childhood and insinuating imagination, in a series of scenes which, moreover, bring us back to the ancient theme of the "upside-down world" (the "roerso" world of certain old Venetian presses). Surrealism, fixed at the opposite pole from the prevalent tendency, onto an almost *figé* rigour, onto an ontologising metaphysic of the word, erupted as a ludic-Dionysian flux, while the other type of expression ended up proposing itself as sacral-Apollonian. Surrealism was therefore more able to produce reverberations in the infantile world. Couplet, series, monorhymed tirade, repetitiveness, parallel verses with partial corrections of meaning, "fake" oral folklore, the worst of childhood doggerel in appearance (sometimes, too, in substance): these are the perpetual scene in the work of the Surrealists, with its fits of "recognition" between signifiers, the glistening of paronomasia and synaesthesia built above foundations made of contiguity and analogical references, with its attachments to "other logics" and fusions and coinages of words; according to this trend, the hyper-sensical sprang very suddenly from nonsense, from the pun sprang the oracular word, and so on. The Surrealist movement didn't have a large or obvious following in Italy; in our panorama it is perhaps the poetry of Gatto which presents itself as the most receptive to this influence, which he takes up only to reject again later in an immediateness of limpid abstraction. The flaming chromatic and acoustic sensibility, if it remains partially inhibited in Gatto's "normal" production, or rather, referred back to an ontic-mental substratum, appears at the height of freedom and collusion in his poetry for children, which stands out clearly in the mediocre panorama of the field.

Out of the same mould, the happy exploits of Rodari develop, who comes to reconnect with Palazzeschi through Prévert and surrealism. In Rodari the restriction of his own poetic act almost exclusively to writing poetry for children—and the option which is implied in this choice—constitute a fact of conscience whose validity reflects through all the poetry of today, a gesture of clarification, a bet placed in a new form of humility and happiness. Even if Rodari speaks of his own poems as though they are "poetic toys" which would only serve as training for higher purposes, and if he states that he is placed at the service of children, not of poetry,[8] in reality he feels the danger now looming of the very cancellation of this last term and he seeks to save it (for others and for himself), precisely pointing it towards the glow of the dawn, vitally making it conscious of that which would be a propaedeutic for it. In Rodari, the yet inevitable insistence on the relation of poetry-infancy (while all the preceding schemes vanish in the *tabula rasa* which was accomplished in the post-war years), in terms of a minimisation of one term or a re-dimensioning of the relation, dares instead to regain the hypothesis, the possibility of a positive project. From childhood as nostalgic, regressive irresponsibility, Rodari turns to childhood as a redemptive nucleus which, resisting every offense, decides to grow, to "respond" to the future, even if this is indecipherable as never before: poetry, transforming itself into a "toy" for this childhood, and situating its own ideal image "elsewhere", which Rodari presumes (for himself) unattainable, will revivify only "as much as it needs to" in the dialogue with the infant.

It is not a coincidence that Rodari himself knew how to graft an articulated thematic of actuality, of concreteness, of fertile sociality (and an efficient didacticism, because intrinsic to these ideals) onto the glistening and fervid fledgling game, rather than taking from Surrealist culture, from the recesses of the psychological and linguistic unconscious sensed in its natural "positivity" (which persists also in its apparent flickering in the void, in its contradictions, negations, "callousnesses" and "tantrums"). It is not a coincidence, because an incarnation of hope—whatever was to be its legitimacy—that it could not but examine itself in terms of so-cial renewal; and Rodari gives us the teacherly smile of a *naturaliter* spirit committed to this renewal, in a spontaneous "socialism" which, less than ideological, was coincident with the capacity to re-find an operative sense of the human in matching the uncircumscribed energies of childhood, a sense that in turn recovers the right words for itself, above all using these words in a highlighted "poetic silhouette".

As we go running through the motives of the "pathetic current" which had its face turned towards the affirmation, in children's poetry, of values of affect and interiority (that are yet not negligible)—with a certain duti-ful "melancholia" in its whispered teaching and teaching solutions, which were just as dutifully optimistic in terms of themes—Rodari testifies for a more courageous and climactic way to enter into this difficult terrain, which is certainly closer to the greater part of the child of today's reality, interior and exterior. Infancy in agricultural and artisan Italy was too much aligned to that pathetic attitude (or, much worse, to reactionary rhetoric with all of its sodden tinsels and stereotypes); now we require something else with a different shape; and finally "the little man in the crane" takes his place among the characters of Pascolian ascendance.

But today, while the worst of the illness is still spreading, is there really a place for any "teacherly smile"? Does every optimism, even minimal, not risk appearing conventional and compulsory?

5. Exactly, we must ask ourselves what the future "is" and what therefore infancy is for the current world, seething with compacted aggression which is both continually erupting and paralysed in an equilibrium of

terror, squashed by the excesses of a population constantly aggravated by the senseless pathological multiplication of needs; while for the majority of humanity, exhausted with hunger, nothing is left except to brandish the Fanonian hatchet. Meanwhile, as occurs in all the other scientific and technological sectors, the human sciences pile up and surround us; there is a vertigo in this, while all the noted formulations of the human come to be destroyed in their deepest foundations, there does not appear to be any that is truly integral and persuasive. We have created a country of fault lines and explosions, of vacuous although formerly audacious structures, of exultant truths together with chalky disenchantment. The "age of anxiety" becomes the era of neurosis and then of psychosis, which are presented as being damaging even if in some way whips, lacklustre; the same innovatory forces, inhibited, tend to reduce themselves to a broken discourse among a myriad of conflicting dogmas, in a fibrillating movement. The crowd, caught between the smoke of the Nazi *lager* and the smoke of the poisoned city-*lagers*, now ends up feeling like a senseless proliferation and malignancy, like a pollution that is the cause of every other pollution.

And thus who does the child become? What will this child of poison be like? How will it react faced with this, the innocent testimony of a fault that is and has been everyone's, today even more than yesterday? Besides, in the time of "birth control", which it is by now necessary to impose by law, the nascent child will not be able to be felt as it was in the past. This figure could be frightening if it comes forth against all schedules, against the empire of preventive reason: but on the contrary, could it conserve the almost charismatic figure that it had, inasmuch as it becomes seen as a "gift" or surprising eruption? And all this without pushing ourselves to consider the interventions of genetics (perhaps these are a little science-fictional although not totally) in determining the characteristics of the child creatures to come. We must ask ourselves what stimuli and what conditionings the idea of the relation of poetry-childhood is about to receive from these unprecedented events.

The problem is much more arduous the more that the uncertainty over the identity of poetry is felt today, over its tasks and significations, the more that people tend to write off its presence as absurd and useless; while poetry itself seems to become "other than itself", almost dissolving itself in the confrontation with other types of artistic reality (even if we cannot describe this in every sense as a process of self-negation). Analogous alterations seem today to countersign, however, poetry and infancy; the "programming of beauty" (Bense and many others) sounds together in a certain way with the programming of the nascent child, with a reduction in both cases in how far we refer back to the invasion of the unforeseen, of the "vital". At the same time the signs are frequent of the "callousness" of culture in relation to the child. It is symptomatic that, in the recent climate of the re-examination of magic and devil-worship, reduced to film-comic book fodder, the child is often not demythologised in an intrepid elucidation in psychoanalytical style, as much as re-mythologised in negative form (nothing like that "wholesomely rebellious" devil-worship, which was spoken of in relation to some figures in infancy-poetry of decades past). According to a bitter illusion that derives from the old demonologies or witch persecution manuals or para-psychological folklore, we allot malign roles to children, those of protagonist or brainwashed or medium. In the American tradition of offering children toys which represent more or less famous monsters—even if we can re-contextualise this in the horrific tradition of fairytales and even if it is already worn out—a tendency towards a form of vendetta against children can be seen. And narrative, at the rather low-cultural level of science fiction and the thriller, but also in high-cultural areas, does not fail to present a distorted image of the child: dwarf, refined criminal, aborted child, mummified foetus or child wisened in old age, an undefinable being, condemned to incommunicability or madness. Regarding this theme, one could go back to the illustrious precedent of *The Turn of the Screw*, contemporary with late-eighteenth-century discoveries about childhood—arriving, in recent times at *Rosemary's Baby*, as the theme is led forward *in excelsis* by its cinematic versions.

And as premonitory, the suicide of Pavese comes to situate itself against these backgrounds, an author who was so passionately engaged in salvaging, both in his prose writings and in his verse, the sorrowful, sweet and savage image of the "boy" (or child), who was so dear to nine-teenth-century tradition. For him "childhood . . . is not that which we were, but that which we always are" (*Feria d'agosto*), and literature is also in-volved in the symptomatic massacre of this innocence, which appears to him sometimes as suicidal consumption, and self-destructive dissipation of the emotional and mythic treasures of childhood, even if after such consumption, he wagers on the resistance of a residual, and re-founding, "autre".[9] Pavese records a suffering, a common life between childhood and the whole of a cultural order; two terms which, however, cannot but be in confrontation.

In inverted terms—even if I enter into an analogous impasse—the child Satan in the cot would show that the origin point is already sick, it is evil, that perhaps "there has never been one" (Artaud).

6. In clear contrast, however, a much larger sector of culture obstinately continues to wager on the child, seeking to know the child and to rec-ognise in it a "scandalous" irreducibility to negation. While the work of psychology departments develops, and as this work is more and more valued and listened to, coordinating with activist and anti-authoritar-ian pedagogies, political research in reformist and revolutionary forms realises more and more openly the truth of what childhood is, in all its potentialities. Lapassade definitively condemns adultism as the most squalid of repressive myths, reminding us that life is always "entrée dans la vie", childhood.[10] Many stories of "saved" boys and girls, or else often of liberators or saviours, speak through the pages of psychoanalytic tracts; like many other children protagonists of comic strips, Mafalda with his fresh rebel consciousness (very different from the "terribleness" of the Gamburrasca tradition) makes us understand many things with

his sentential flashes onto reality. And a—yet disputable—journal such as *Re Nudo*, referring to the Andersen-esque child who has the courage to deny the existence of the "Emperor's New Clothes", takes the infancy that calls things by their real name as an emblem, because it loves and generates truth even when fantastic, creating its "own" myths.

This culture also knows how to grasp the suggestions coming from the world of the "enfants sauvages", whose atrocious destiny confirms the incredible plasticity of the human psyche, even allowing us to glimpse in man an "absence of nature" which is also the possibility for ever new "creations of nature" (as hinted at in Malson's essay).[11] Moreover, attention towards "enfants prodiges" is emphasised here, and G. Doman, who teaches children to read by the age of three, almost directs them all on their way to becoming such a figure. Leopardi's verses for children, wasted, thanks to Maria Corti, on a popular newspaper, appear to us as allusion to a limitless vital force, potentially paradisiac, which burned in the most credited representative of pessimism "of the text": the irony of an almost Mozartian infantile-celestial Arcadia lying in the stink of the daily chronicle. Silvio Ceccato clarifies, even to himself, his own logical and cybernetic theories in his conversation with children.[12]

As for our most recent poetry, even amid the nightmares, it has continued to keep its eye on infancy, on a subterranean level, in a sometimes dissimulating and insecure way. Already along the paths of psychoanalysis and linguistics, *babil*, the language of nursing and suckling, dialect as the true parlance of many children or of the self-same poets in the time of their childhood (the case of Pasolini's "frut" can stand in for all here), sing-song (always related to exorcism); these assume in certain poetry of today the value of points of emergence, of ovules in the field in which negation has been, at least, put in doubt. Even if in such positions we are not lacking Twilight or Pascolian influences, there is all the same in these positions the durability of a defensive tic and also of an ethical imperative which becomes one with this. In a tragic mixture of aphasia, references, resignations, these elements are greeted as a "responsibility", they respond immediately, they become the solitary melodies in a universe of screeches closed in its blinding and blinded activism "which does not respond". Other authors instead, such as the "visual-technologists" Pignotti and Micini, salvage certain poetic-infantile materials through ironic resumption and changing their contexts, strategies which neo-capitalistic advertising has gripped hold of, well knowing their primordial persuasive (softening) powers; these come to align with children that, placed in front of television advertising of this type, succeed in innocently catching it like a song, to transform it into poetry, even if it is not really this, if it is counterfeit.

As for poetic production which is addressed towards infancy, it is said that Rodari stands on the dividing line where this kind of production does not distinguish itself from the other kind, gesturing to a line of resistance and advance, inasmuch as under the suspicion of conventionality which today, further, is intrinsic to every human gesture. Examples in this line are not lacking: Rodari himself appears alongside Arpino, Landolfi, Santucci and others in the collection *Nuove filastrocche*; a scholar such as E. Petrini poses an analogous terrain of poetic research with positive results; Adriana Giussani tries the "animated book" in which verses have a notable function. But, if in the field of narrative and prose we see a flourishing of "updated" but not unworthy works (while collections multiply, graphically well-curated and rich with modern figurative material, as we can see in the international exhibition of Children's Books which happens yearly in Bologna), in poetry one has the impression that everything considered, the brooding of tender-rural themes prevails, even in certain collections for winning entries to competitions for unpublished writers, which then struggle to find a publisher. However, far from secondary, the problem of reconciliation exists, between more "realistic" needs (even in poetry) and those of fantasy and sentiment, because the child needs to be spared from the danger of premature forms or excessive disenchantment, which moreover is often imposed on it by its environment.

Passion and perplexity, decisions to act and defeatism, conscious alarm and archaic illusions characterise then, in contradictory ways, the behaviour of the pedagogical world of today in relation to poetry, whose determining presence in the educative act, connected with the other branches of experience and knowledge, one can recognise. And the antinomies of the poetic act, we might argue, come to be confused with those of the pedagogical act, of this firing area of cultural work which appears more than ever to be labouring under the sign of Sisyphus. Investigations of poetry in school are not lacking, even if they are not numerous, and they reveal a differentiated situation, between uncertainties, contrasts, discouragements and slightly facile optimisms, both in Italy and elsewhere. The two French works cited in the notes to the beginning of this essay are particularly rich in data; also interesting are the enquiries conducted by the journal *Cahiers Pédagogiques*[13] and by I. Drago, to whom we owe among other things a meticulous, precise panorama of poetry for children in Italy, even if imposed on it are criteria which are in part questionable;[14] worth meditating on is the conversation between pupils and teacher brought by L. Muraro Vaiani in *L'erba voglio*,[15] the collection of talks on social-pedagogical experiences; also *Liuba*—thirty-five nineteenth-century Italian poets illustrated and commented on by children—, edited by M. Ghirardelli, it is a timely anthology and of the most sincere interest, even if it manifests a certain methodological imprecision.[16] In the meantime, schools enrich their audio-visual media and other didactic aides, which are always more and more valid and efficient, even in presenting poetry and in growing the capacity for "irradiation". Thanks to these means poetry will better come to be understood "ut pictura" and as "musique encore et toujours"; there it will reap in its essence "idea harmony image—aura of fertile love" (to speak with Tommaseo), or much more, or even much less, but it will have an experience which counts for something. Poetry, which today accompanies few people beyond childhood or at least beyond school age, will last, perhaps, as a longer echo in souls, even while it will continue to be scrutinised in a wider field by the harsh re-examination which is being made of its position in nursery-school, in society and, of course, in the cosmos . . .

Even the myth of the "poetic anthology" should be thought through more deeply, re-thought and at last overcome. The discourse on the anthology is not a vain one, but it comes from a gnawing need-stubbornness which derives from sources far away from *désir* and of a certain "pragmatic sentiment", no less than the discourse on the encyclopaedia. For this the concerns of Cantu or Sailer (*La vispa Teresa* . . .) merit consideration (already now in the last century—or later, of Lipparini or Plona or of the same Drago); concerns to create anthologies for children, which were well-received, as numerous others were, and to which we could add, under the deity Pascoli, the anthologies for middle-school especially the often notably well-developed poetic parts of them. It is this sector which is changing; and the choices in these anthologies can in certain cases value at least as outlines for that anthology which conscious educators can and must "locate" with all their strength, according to the particular needs of the pupils; with their participation to find more appropriate selections made from as various and broad materials as possible. Neither should we absolutely consider superfluous an outline for a new anthology which would be the fruit of a work of *équipe* (sociologists, scholars of letters, pedagogues, linguists, psychologists, etc.) and of a survey of the enjoyment which its recipients get from it.

There also exists a space for children's theatre, in which to retrain ourselves, in joining theatre to the experience of poetry;[17] and to be re-invented, according to Benjamin, by the sons of the proletariat, those on whom the construction of a human future will especially depend—if there should be one—or by those little Morante children to whom we owe the salvation of the world. Poetry—reactivated in this current of theatre which is "low" but which is in the first instance the action of the children themselves, a psychodrama in its deconditioning and therapeutic opening-out—could re-find a centrality which has been long lost and become truly choral, something wished even by the Surrealists. This chorality, rooted in the popular *couche*, would also be better able to value the rich traditions of dialect poetry, both in its nameless voices which reflect the feelings and the experiences of the masses back and forth across the centuries, as well as in texts which are more properly literary. Regional and peasant microcosms, certainly not dead in Italy, in the freshness of their passions, among which the infantile theme always finds emphasis, could also in this way become harmonised, avoiding every traumatic opposition to culture "in the language". In such a process the work of Pierro or Giotti, of Dell'Arco or di Guerra or di Noventa or of the already mentioned Pasolini (a few names at random) would have the important place that they deserve. In this area, we might better value that poetry which, developing itself around the Romantic period and which persisted for most of the nineteenth century, was inspired by popular rhythmic patterns and motifs, well enjoyed by children for its singable quality: certain translations found success, for example those of Goethe, Heine, Platen, all the better if a bit "dated" (Carducci's of the *Tomba del Busento!*), or compositions such as *La leggenda di Teodorico*[18] or parodies like *Il prode Anselmo*.

We are talking, then, of a sunburst of convergences—to which we might add many more, including broader interdisciplinary additions—in which the only thing that is ever realised is the educative act; convergences which it is almost impossible to actualise in the asphyxiated situation of the contemporary nursery-school, held by many now to be a noxious, lifeless simulacrum, that must be swept away.[19] It will however be better to focus, minimally, on its necessary transformation and integration on a global scale (see the recent report of UNESCO).[20]

We must also continue to concede a little sense to a kind of poetic research which becomes better and better at incorporating children, which can do so thanks to them, and which keeps in mind that they are waiting for something but especially that they give something, unthinkably new, for the sole reason that they exist. The child is already in the future, it will be other than that which we are: for this reason—just what we want to hear—it is always a Jesus among the doctors.

It is true that the un-placeable figure which is still today called poet (by now on the brink of erasure?) is turned towards explaining in its particularly intense way, even by the equivocal light of Narcissus, "that which is to come" and becomes exposed to the radiations of the "outside", touching something of which nothing has yet been said; we are talking about a minute fragment of reality. Poetry and infancy in this unsaid will come to speak to us; the risk that it will be terrible, on a horizon in which revelation and apocalypse could etymologically coincide, cannot justify a refusal to listen. In another sense, as Montale seems to want to tell us in the explicit of his *Diario del '71*, the poet cannot ever be the chiliast of everything, cannot ever truly profess a doctrine of *finis mundi*. Again, the child and the poet (or solely some poets?) continue to find themselves in the overflowing, lush aura of wonder, rediscovering in it sparks and reliefs of events which to many are imperceptible, recalling other people to it. They are located, as has always been the case, in the wonder which builds the always new feeling of being new, open to the trauma of admirration-anguish, capable of reorganising everything around a nucleus of awakening which gives rise to the future, futurises the past and the present removing them from that fold of duress which they tend to fall back into and to freeze. In a time said—and in many ways rightfully—to be one of misery and dejection, hypnotised by fatuous possible futures (as in the worst science fiction) that are overlaid and which mutually cancel each other—the act of recognition which can still occur between poetry and infancy cannot but allude to the ignition of a sheaf of wildly different hypotheses, to the activation of a "deliberate" image of rediscovered authenticity. It is an uncertain light, contested, blocked, maybe tired by now; but it is one of the very few that remain.

(1973)

NOTES

*These notes appear in the original as page footnotes, not together as endnotes here.
Some minor adjustments have been made to bibliographic citations so that they conform
more closely to usual English and French practices, which differ from Italian—ed.*

[1] Important also in this regard are the recent works: J. Charpentrau, *Enfance et poésie* (Paris, Ed. Ouvrières, 1972); J. P. Gourévitch, *Les Enfants et la poésie* (Paris, Ed. de l'Ecole, 1969), which are cited in a study conducted previously by P. Juif, P. Giscard, etc.

[2] cf. Primaur, Lhong and Malrieu, *Le Mythe de l'enfance dans la literature contemporaine* (Paris, PUF, 1961).

[3] cf. G. Petter, *Conversazioni psicologiche con gli insegnanti* (Florence, Giunti–Barbera, 1971), pp. 254–75.

[4] This is a theme which effectively lends itself to misunderstanding, because there also exists a problem of "introduction to creativity" (there is an immense literature in this vein). But it would not be wrong to underscore the exaltation of infantile creativity which appears, for example, in the report of the "Mouvement du 22 mars 1968".

[5] It is enough to cite, among the many, the examples listed in: M. Lodi, *Il paese sbagliato* (Turin, Einaudi, 1970); on the basis of a type of experimentation which is alive enough in the Freinet school.

[6] "E quando potei cantare: padre che ci hai tenuto sui ginocchi . . . Il vecchio morì veramente in quel punto" [And when I could speak: father that kept us on our knees . . . The old man truly died at that moment]; in the "strip" *Evasione.*

[7] cf. M. David, *La psicoanalisi nella cultura italiana* (Turin, Boringhieri, 1966), p.423.

[8] cf. G. Rodari, "I bambini e la poesia", in *Il giornale dei genitori* (Milan, June 1972).

[9] cf. J. Hösle, "I miti dell'infanzia", in the work of Pavese, in *Sigma*, 3–4 (Turin, 1964), partial translation of J. Höde, *Cesare Pavese* (Berlin, De Gruyter, 1961).

[10] cf. G. Lapassade, *L'Entrée dans la vie* (Paris, Ed. de Minuit, 1963).

[11] L. Malson, *Les Enfants sauvages* (Paris, Ed. 10/18, 1964). On this theme cf. also Truffaut's film, with the story of the boy Victor de l'Aveyron.

[12] S. Ceccato, *Il maestro inverosimile*, 2 vols (Milan, Bompiani, 1972).

[13] *Cahiers Pédagogiques*, nos. 99, 101 (Biarritz, & Paris 1971).

[14] I. Drago, *La poesia per ragazzi in Italia* (Florence, Giunti, Bemporad, Marzocco, 1972), p. 97n.

[15] L. Muraro Vaiani, "A che serve la poesia?," in: AA.VV., *L'erba voglio* (Turin, Einaudi, 1971); the study conducted in this volume is now continued in the very lively and advanced journal of the same name.

[16] AA.VV., *Liuba* (Milan, Mursia, 1972).

[17] A theatrical adaptation of Rodari's *La Torta in cielo* was presented, with his poetry inserted, by R. Milani, and it had a resounding success at the Festival of Children's Cinema and Theatre in Venice. We must also remember the theatrical action *La mia tua la sua la nostra la vostra la loro*, integrated with poetry by Ginsberg, performed by the II B class of the "Quasimodo" middle school of the Vallette (Turin) and later presented again in the same venue.

[18] G. Rodari, *I bambini e la poesia*, cit.

[19] cf. Ivan Illich, *Deschooling Society* (New York, Harper and Row, 1971); E. Reimer, *School is Dead* (Harmonsworth, Penguin Education Specials, 1971).

[20] AA.VV., *Apprendre à être* (Paris, UNESCO–Fayard, 1972).

"Infanzie, Poesie, Scuoletta (appunti)" in
Andrea Zanzotto, *Fantasie di Avvicinamento* (Milan, Mondadori, 1991)
first printed in *Strumenti critici*, no. 20 (Turin, Einaudi, February 1973)

SOANDANG KIM YEON

WRITING PAINTINGS

opposite: Nevertheless, black ink, blue surround, pale red flower, 350 x 450 mm
first spread left: Find the Way, black ink, deep red flower, 340 x 350 mm
first spread right: Dream, black and brown ink, red nose, 600 x 430 mm
second spread left: Tranquil Life, black ink, brown beak, 510 x 400 mm
second spread right: Draw the Moon, black ink, red rabbit, pestle and mortar, 340 x 400 mm
last: Life as a Series of Challenges, black ink, red fruit, small red flower on left,
small red bird and showerhead on right, 345 x 410 mm

Nevertheless is dated 2011, the others are dated 2010, all paintings include red seals

the calligraphic legends in Nevertheless, Dream, Life as a Series of Challenges
are drawn from classical Korean literature
the calligraphic legends in Find the Way, Tranquil Life, Draw the Moon
are the Soandang's own

————

With grateful thanks to Sung Hee Jin for assistance

마음으로 얻어낸
바가는

젊신발생삶을속히쓰지삶을불다쓰고갔다삶을꼭설받쓰를쓴현생처럼살겠었다나는몇번을   한한두끼돈양양하앙이아양속일엇위가얼은하왔어너하위근엇잎밠생있

[74]

DOROTHY LEHANE

Six Poems

CARRINGTON EVENT

there's going to be a geomagnetic judder
knocking out pacemakers, incubators & dialysis,
don't sass me over freedom to outline, flesh façade
of wild mess & woes; oh, *you'll never get to heaven
in a ping pong ball*, you're subterranean with that smile
ending the first half of my life with a bang in l'état moteur.
I find the endgame, a hairpin turn, *he's out at sea,
she's ashore*, keep this in a joint archive, psycho-state
with flat-footed questions, recognise absence toward
every other human, no choice but to write Ibsen's
next play & the new article for my mother—
vibrating at 'oh my, that's wonderful' an obelisk
tapering off & terminating with at least three children
& why the hell shouldn't the subatomic look pretty

CARRYING CAPACITY

celebrate the anniversary
of a dead friend
        her absence of being
post rigor/
        w/ three epithets
byname-by-byname
harvest nostalgia
with local humour

it is a fact that the tongue
is an early warning system
of both taste & character

Whisky in Orbit

I have used bayesian mathematics
to map what you'll say next
the whisky is radiated
make what you must of this
there is a degree of wakefulness
when speech falls into new use
I cachéd vignettes of you
the thickness of your thumb
you leave the lyrical door open
join the necropolis or don't
sacré nom de Dieu
you render me over-exposed
tales of ancient mariners
& mermaids & goddamn it
I am barely capable of utterance
distilling all this will take years

CODA

post alcoholic phrases in free-wheel
accept the vow as negative valence
absence in pseudo-scientific terms
a letter to the ash dryads asking
for a little sweet talk in the nascent state
bring the behaviour of the glottis
its frozen-brother-sister-language
to the fore; scanning embryo speech
for lesions, for behavioural catch-phrases
glosses from birth to sectarian theatre;
all patients over his chronology
coup de grâce at the throat

Retrieval States

oh my darling,, oh my darling clementine
the more mitigating the circumstances
the more it behoves me to listen //
in the blanker regions of my constitution
I've gained the rank of battleaxe

      wheel in a new threshold
I was no swimmer,, dreadful sorry
we converge over sorry,, elicit slips
in the buffer stage,, our transient problem
is unlikely language

        —goes some way under lesioned conditions,,
this versus // my mulberry morpheme
by the latencies,, age of acquisition
in a cavern,, in a canyon
           unreformattable we double up
   all or none //

BRAIDED

there's no being closer to me
than helping my wayward angular gyrus
recall repartee   :   girlhood versus
                    the corpus of dull
&, in its abeyance
far more than muted tension
// stress signal
enduring the minus hours
            past the furore of outpouring
happy in your orgy
—your scansion, (((girl in wellspring))
so much to let in
reading long before light
your craft   you, new lover
we go as far as
total-body
total-plexus

STEFANO PASTOR

FOUR SCORES FROM UNCRYING SKY

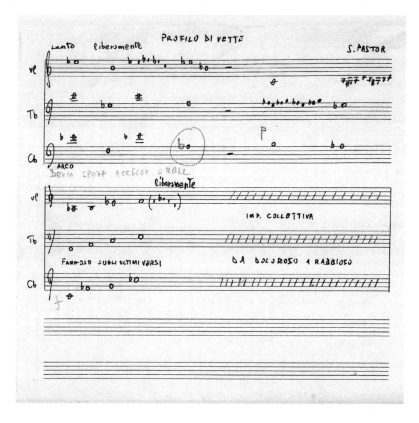

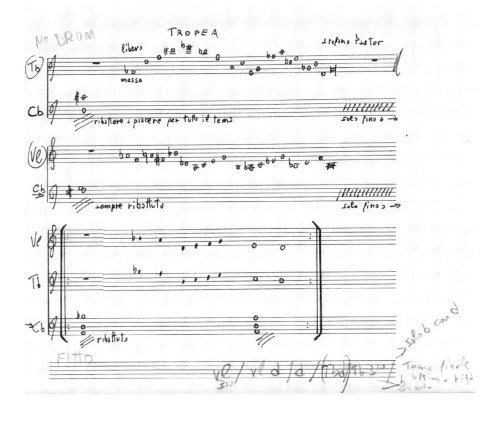

Four of eight compositions for improvisation inspired by the composer's
poems, which are printed with English transliterals in the liner notes to
Uncrying Sky, CD Silta SR0702, Recorded Milan, 29 January 2007
Stefano Pastor vn, Giancarlo Schiaffini tb, Giorgio Dini bs, Daviano Rotella dm

ALEXANDRA SASHE

5 POEMS

Dividing the meadows with a monastic short step
                              without a wake
a snowed-under path between
the vine- and the grave-yard
          past Würzburg, a ladder of January.

With burnt hands carrying flames
immaculate black
            sackcloth and ashes in bloom
            the garment of soleness in unison with the wind.

carrying time across the bridge,
across the estuary of Lethe.

ADVENTAL

A word whispered to a vine stalk—
at a quarter to the first hour.
barrels of water, rain's cousins,
hem the vineyard in chronological order.

A word-whisper come from the Jordan
curtails the wine's time-long way to bleeding.
A dry kneaded bread face to face with a child's beginning.
Water conveys the secret of its sanguine being.
The child dies back into the quarter past his beginning—
and is reborn
               unleavened.

No wind. The slowed down clock may let go of its
straw- and tear-woven towers,
recover its breath.   The north moves nowhere from the field
of vision and holds on with one fast finger
to the one sole promise
the towers left
in their wake.

They grow green, inaccessible to the upturned faces that
time now breathes out at long intervals. The space between
their sleep and wake disappears, and they are about
about to fly
to retrace their steps by way
of where the north
and the promise
lie.

A Tear

And if I don't cry—where
do I look for it,
where
do my knees become one with the ground,
and crows cleave
into my speechless,
into the taut
cords of the violins

And if a tear holds fast
and saltless,
if
it presumes limpidity, if
I obey the tear's presumption,

where do I look for my knees and the ground
in their orphan-like
separation

And still, should the knees
and the ground forgive me
and come
into their inheritance,
                            will I
be naked enough
to be crows and violins
and disinherit myself

from the tear ?

(And if the seasalt and brine of the spoken
come to pass
through the millennial layers,
will they suffice
to enter the tear,

and will I suffice
for a single tear,

and will
this tear suffice?)

LENTEN

And if the daylight
prevails in my vessel, and hands
prevailed upon with the weight
of the scent
of mimosa and acquiescence,

I wake up in a clean month
with a monstrance space
behind my chest.

Tear summons its secrecy, salt
imparts to the eye its saltness. A windless week
becomes a kingdom.

And if I confide in the fluid and simple
and measure with hours my calendar,

It is a penultimate day of completion.

Fruit lives by its juice
I taste on my knees
        and host on my palm.

Its kernel sister to tear.

The looking glass pays out the years
stored overnight behind
        its amalgam.

                And if I confide in its golden
                warp and weft
                of skins and kernels,

the month of April knows
the value (qualified and added
by the thaw water) of

a tear.

GUNNAR EKELÖF

translated from the Swedish by

ANTHONY BARNETT

Voices Under the Earth

The hours pass. Time passes.
It is late or early for different people.
It is late or early for different light.
—Silently the morning light jars the drug of sleep
and shelves it away in all the pharmacies
(with their black-white-checkered floors)—
colourless and dawn-bitter
myself tired as never years and days until death . . .
—I long from the black square to the white.
—I long from the red thread to the blue.

That young man! (there is something wrong with his face)—
That pale girl! (her hand is in the flowers at the window:
she exists only together with her hand
which only exists together with . . .)
The bird that flies and flies. With its flight.
Someone who hides. Others who only exist together with the other.
The old woman sneaking around and around until she is discovered.
Then slyly smiling she turns and retires.
But she comes back.
The caretaker at the desk (stained in well-worn pinegrain). He has no eyes.
The child turned toward the blackboard, always turned to the blackboard.

The pointer's screech. Where is the hand?
It is in the flowers at the window.
The smell of chalk. What does the smell of chalk say to us?
That the hours pass, time passes.
That slowly the morning light pulverizes the drug of sleep . . .
. . . with their black-white-checkered floors—

Archaeopteryx! What a lovely name!
Archaeopteryx! My bird!
—Why does it chirrup so unhappily?
—It chirrups about its life, wants to fly away, has perhaps already flown.
I have already fondled it as a stone.
With thousand-year beats my stone heart beat in my veins.
Perhaps there were petrified birds and lizards in there!
Rhamphornycus! Archaeopteryx!
In a new light the stone became a living bird and flew off
but now and then out of duty or habit it comes back.
Someone is always left behind, that is the horror.
—Iguanodon!
The bird is gone but says it is still here—is that to protect itself?
How can it still be here? It is not here. It is you who are still here.
The bird is free. It is you who wait.
I wait.
I long for the bird that flies and flies
with its flight.
Myself I am bound to the stone. The age-old stone.

Lately the bird has complained that it cannot sleep.
Who can sleep?
I woke the bird one night—it was indoors.
I woke it because my thoughts were plaguing me.

I wanted to know.
The bird says it flies away in order to give me a much greater happiness—
A diplomatic fight for freedom!
I fondled a stone. I became a stone.
I was the last piece in the jigsaw
the piece that didn't fit anywhere, the picture complete without me.
Something is always left over, that is the horror.
Everything turned inside out in me, everything vaporized.
The bird took my wings and gave them to another light.
It went out. It was dark.
Archaeopteryx! Archaeopteryx!
I groped around me, got nothing in my hands
nothing to remember, nothing to forget . . .
—Is there no forgetfulness in the house of the abyss?
—Not when everything is abyss.
—Is there no light?
—Not when it is out.
—Is it day or night?
—It is night.
—How hard the lamps stare!
—They watch over the stones.
—So far below the surface!
—There is no surface.
But there, on the bed, I see a solitary limestone among the fish . . .
Deaf, dumb they circle around in their own light.
It has no light.
It has no bed.
It cannot close its eyes over someone's joy.
It cannot open them.
—This is hell!
—No, it is emptiness.

And the house of the stars is empty
and the souls
draw away from the universe—
Slowly and indifferently the earth wraps time around its axis,
more tensile than some elastic band.
Your feet have to take the endlessly winding spiral staircase,
the stair spindle that twists dizzily like a wide-eyed dream
from landing to landing, from stair-tread to stair-tread of stone . . .
You hold your head still:
You are forced to take the stair-treads one at a time and your body twists:
You twist your head.
You suffocate in stone, suspended in viscous stone, in which you sleep.
Birds and molluscs sleep there like you
with lizards and flowers,
and even raindrops sleep
on pillows of stone, under sheets of stone.
With thousand year beats their hearts of stone beat
in veins of stones.
For a billion billion years time swirls them with itself
in raging storms of stones through seas of stone
to skies of stone . . .
—What am I? Where are you?
—Wake up!
—In the house of the abyss.
—Is there no obliviousness in the house of the abyss?
—Not one's own but others'.
And all these homeless patients who drift around the day rooms
have only walls for doctors.
A zigzag of temperature charts covers the barred off doors.
Everything lies on its back, everything turns
again and again on its back. No one knows

what is up or down. Everything turns
again and again on its back,
even the chairs, even walls and floors.
Everything turns.
Everyone's eyes are blank and as empty as windows,
one sees neither night nor day . . .
—Is it night or day?
—It is night
and the night rests mirroring and black against the windowpanes.
The night rises, the night is soon on the fourth floor.
The night is soon on the fifth floor.
The night is soon on the sixth floor.
Now the night is on the seventh floor.
—How many floors are there?
—A lot.
—What tremendous pressures against the windowpanes on the ground floor!
Should they shatter the night would rush in,
fill the rooms with darkness, rise from floor to floor!
—Keep to the side up there on the stairs!
—What's with the push and shove!
—No tarrying!
There is a throbbing in the radiators as if a heart were straining,
the lamps go dead when they act out the opposite
and try to hold back the darkness.
A white loneliness against a black loneliness.
Or a black loneliness against a white loneliness.
And while the darkness swirls round the gables of the house
from all these lonelinesses comes cry after cry of silence:
—Who are you, shadow at the pine-stained desk?
—Death was left sitting at his place like a wretched caretaker.

The hours pass. Time passes.
Slowly the morning light pulverizes the drug of sleep.
—I long from the black square to the white.
—I long from the red thread to the blue.

"Röster under jorden" from "Två fristående dikter" in
Om hösten (Stockholm, Bonniers, 1951) reprinted in a.o.
Skrifter 1: Dikter 1927–1951 (Stockholm, Bonniers, 1991)

The image of the archaeopteryx does not accompany this poem
but appears as the last page of Ekelöf's *En Mölna-elegi: Metamorfoser*
(Stockholm, Bonniers, 1960) reprinted in a.o.
Skrifter 2: Dikter 1955–1962 (Stockholm, Bonniers, 1991)

From Things to Sounds

Very odd transactions are underway just now in my vicinity. In my ears I still hear the Prime Minister's raised, adamantine cadence: "No, not even a thirty!" from the car in which he sits with the door open onto the curb, in a dress suit, as my newfound friend, who calls him his "quarter-uncle" and who is son to some other kind of bigwig, leans down over the car door in an attempt to borrow money off him, while asking me to move a few steps to one side. I think: he's not shy that one. One sort of society is no better than the other.

I would not have allowed myself to remain in such a faux situation if I had not just gone arm in arm with his sister. She is delightful, trusting, utterly unspoilt, and her evening gown, her soft, shiny, well-groomed hair bun about her neck (1939 model), do nothing but add perverse touches to the aura she has around her of a log driver's bride from Ådalen. Now that she's standing obliquely in front of me on the gardens' path I can most discreetly cast a caressing glance at her back. Compared with her brother there is really nothing to be said.

A little later in the evening I am sitting alone, very much alone, in a kind of round ivory tower, like a villa tower on top of a wooden house, in the midst of composing music. I have an instrument somewhere but I hear the music around me, how it rises, towering up, building ever higher and higher. It is a two-tone orchestral piece, part of a symphony, the relationship between the keys is more-or-less C sharp minor for the left hand and B flat major for the right. It sounds as if I had Bach in my right hand, a slow solemn Bach, and a Swedish folk air in my left hand, a funny sort of Swedish folk air. As I said, it is a sketch for a symphony and there and then I think up the legend: "Puisque vous ne voulez que de grandes machines, en voici un éléphant!"

Now that gives me more of a whiff of the Hector Berlioz'. But when I woke up, even with the music in my head, it was another thing all together, I do remember.

EUPHORIA

You sit in the garden alone with a notebook, a sandwich, flask and pipe.
It is night but so calm that the light burns without flickering,
spreads its reflection over the table of rough-hewn planks
and glistens in the bottle and the glass.

You take a draught, a bite, you fill and light your pipe.
You write a line or two and pause a moment to contemplate
the streak of sunset red sailing toward the morning red,
the sea of wild chervil, a green-white foam in the summer night's dusk,
not a single moth around the light but choruses of gnats in the oak,
leaves so still against the sky . . . And the aspen that rustles in the
    stillness:
All nature strong with the love and death around you.

As if this were the last evening before a long, long voyage:
The ticket is in one's pocket and the packing is done.
And you can sit and sense the distant land's closeness,
sense how everything is in everything, at the same time its end and its
    beginning,
sense that here and now are both leavetaking and homecoming,
sense how death and life are strong like the wine within you!

Yes, to be one with the night, one with myself, with the light's flame
as it looks me quietly in the eyes, unfathomable and quiet,
one with the aspen rustling and whispering,
one with the flocks of flowers leaning out of the darkness and listening
to something I had on the tip of my tongue to say that never got said,
something I don't want to let out even if I could.
And that murmurs within me of the purest joy!

And the flame rises . . . As if the flowers pressed closer,
closer and closer in shimmering flecks of rainbow.
The aspen quivers and dances, the evening red sails
and everything that was unsayable and distant is unsayable and close.

   I sing of the only thing that syncretizes,
   the only practical, for all alike.

Non Serviam

I am a stranger in this land
but this land is no stranger in me!
I am not at home in this land
but this land behaves as if it were at home in me!

     ✳

I have in me a blood that can never be diluted
a tumbler full in my veins!
And always the Jew, the Lapp, the artist in me
seeks his blood brother: searches in the writings
makes a detour round the seite in the wilderness
in wordless reverence for something forgotten
joik in the wind: Savage! Nigger!—
butt and shout at the stones; Jew! Black!—
outside the law and within the law:
imprisoned in theirs, the Whites, and still
—praise be my law!—in mine!

Thus I have become a stranger in this land
but this land has made itself at ease in me!
I cannot live in this land
but this land lives like bane in me!

Once, in the brief, the mild
the poor whiles' wild Sweden
there was my land! It was everywhere!
Here, in the long, the well-fed whiles'
tight and cosy Sweden
where everything is sealed against draughts . . . to me it's cold.

———

"Non serviam" and
"From things to sounds" title in English in the original
from "Dikter vid skilda tillfällen 1930–45" in
Non servium (Stockholm, Bonniers, 1945) reprinted in a.o.
Skrifter 1: Dikter 1927–1951 (Stockholm, Bonniers, 1991)
Glossary to "Non Serviam"
seite Sami ancient cult stone
joik Sami traditional song style

"Eufori" from "Fuga" in
Färjesång (Stockholm, Bonniers, 1941) reprinted in a.o.
Skrifter 1: Dikter 1927–1951 (Stockholm, Bonniers, 1991)

See Anthony Barnett, "Antonym: Gunnar Ekelöf's Table" in
Tears in the Fence, 59 (spring 2014) for an overview of translations of Ekelöf

BRIDGET PENNEY

THE HUNTER

. . . when, for instance, he ascended the grand staircase and entered 'the Painted
Room' with its gilt mouldings and its panels painted with subjects from Ovid,
including the Actaeon and Stag over the mantel-piece, with the swan which he
himself had added to the picture . . .

> Thomas Wright, *Isaac Watts and Contemporary Hymn-Writers*

Muse, view the Paintings, how the hovering Light
Plays o're the Colours in a wanton Flight,
And mingled Shades wrought in by soft Degrees
Give a sweet Foyl to all the Charming Piece;

> Isaac Watts, *A Funeral Poem on Thomas Gunston Esq.*

So raught she water in her hand and for to wreak the spite
Besprinkled all the head and face of this unlucky knight
And thus forespake the heavy lot that should upon him light,
'Now make thy vaunt among thy mates, thou saw'st Diana bare.
Tell if thou can; I give thee leave. Tell hardly, do not spare.'
This done, she makes no further threats but by and by doth spread
A pair of lively old hart's horns upon his sprinkled head.
She sharps his ears; she makes his neck both slender, long and lank;
She turns his fingers into feet, his arms to spindle-shank.
She wraps him in a hairy hide beset with speckled spots
And planteth in him fearfulness.

> Ovid, trans. Arthur Golding (1567) *Metamorphoses*, Bk 3, lines 224–234

IN THE PREFACE to his *Loves of the Plants* (1791) Erasmus Darwin refers
to Ovid as 'a great Necromancer' who 'did by art poetic transmute Men,
Women, and even Gods and Goddesses . . .' Apart from Actaeon's, what
other metamorphoses might have been represented on the panels of the
painted room in Abney House? That of Daphne, caught by Apollo as
her feet take root and her limbs harden into branches. Or Arachne—who

in weaving a cheeky tapestry of the shape changes effected by Jove in his pursuit of mortal girls could almost stand for Ovid himself—at the instant when Minerva, fed up with her boasting, turns her into a spider. Possibly the moment Pygmalion returns home after praying in the temple of Venus for a wife resembling the ivory statue he has carved. He extends his fingers to the statue's breast and, in response, she quickens into life.

Trees, spiders and statues are all very much present in the 'managed wilderness' of Abney Park today. There is even a small herd of fallow deer in an enclosure at Clissold Park, five minutes' walk away. Shy and cute, apart from during the rutting season when the stink of the stags hangs in the air, they do their best to lose themselves when the grass is long, an occasional dappled fawn uncamouflaging for an audience more interested in Bambi than Actaeon.

When Thomas Gunston started work on the building that would, much later, become known as Abney House, Isaac Watts was living next door at Fleetwood House as tutor to the children of Sir John Hartropp. The story goes that Watts added the swan to the picture of Actaeon and the stag one day while the artist was at lunch. After Gunston's death at the age of thirty-four in October 1700, his sister Lady Mary Abney inherited the property. Watts would live there, as the Abney family's guest, for the last sixteen years of his life until his own death in 1748. Describing '*the painted room*, on which very considerable expense must have been lavished' in *Cemetery Interment* (1840), George Collison, one of the directors of the company who transformed the contiguous grounds of Abney House and Fleetwood House into London's first non-denominational garden cemetery, additionally mentions 'On the window-shutters are some pictorial delineations which are said to be the production of Watts's pencil, and are intended as emblematic of death and grief, with the Gunston and Abney arms painted under the respective figures.'

Writing at least ten years after Abney House had been demolished, the Rev. John Stoughton in his *Shades and Echoes of Old London* encourages his readers to take a carefully-managed imaginative leap. 'Wait for a moment here, in what is called the painted room. It is moulded in gilt, with panels enclosing pictures, the subjects taken from the poems of Ovid. But in the window shutters are some strange contrasts with these heathen embellishments; for there, contributed, we are told, by Watts's pencil (the poet being an artist too), are emblems of grief and death, mingled with the arms of Gunston and Abney, and intended doubtless to honour their memory.' And a description of the long-vanished room in Edward Walford's *Old and New London* (1878) perpetuates this mid-nineteenth century evangelical disapproval of Ovid by the close verbal borrowing 'heathenish embellishments'. Yet Anna Maria Fielding Hall, who writes about her own visit to the house in 1842, shortly before its demolition, and, from her form elsewhere, would have felt the need to explain the paintings from the *Metamorphoses* had she considered their presence to be any kind of inappropriate anomaly, merely footnotes her account in *Pilgrimages to English Shrines*. '. . . [T]here was one "painted room" on the first floor, the panels of which were filled with landscapes and figures, and which must have originally been gorgeous in effect'.

Gunston must have enjoyed his friend's intervention on the Actaeon picture since the swan stayed to be pointed out to generations of visitors. I assume it glided across the pool in which Diana and her attendants, hot and tired—like Actaeon himself—after a long morning's hunting, were bathing. Ovid describes the relief and pleasant anticipation with which Diana puts aside her weapons and takes off her shoes and leggings; one of her attendants pins up the goddess's hair while leaving her own unbound. Their bathing place is a naturally formed fountain within a dark grove of pines and cypresses. Golding's translation of 'with pineapple and cypress trees' (Bk 3, line 179) reads bizarrely at first, but Francis Bacon's essay *On Gardens* (1625) recommends, 'for the climate of London', 'such things as are green all winter: Holly, Ivy, Bays, Juniper, Cypress-trees, Yew, Pineapple-trees, Fir-trees' which suggests pine cones were the original pineapples and the tropical fruit was named for a resemblance imagined to them. On such a hot day in the forest the smell of pine resin would have been exhilarating and sickly. The lack of undergrowth would have made it easy to walk between the tree trunks but, where there were no clear paths, every direction could have felt the same.

Actaeon's discovery of Diana and her attendants has provided painters with an unrivalled opportunity for the display of female flesh. It's hard to imagine the girls in Titian's *Diana and Actaeon* (1556–9) running for a bus, let alone chasing deer all morning in the ever-increasing heat. Scrutinising this picture of the moment of discovery, I share in Actaeon's fault—and am much more culpable, because Ovid stressed that the hunter 'ranging in the wayless woods' (Bk 3, line 171) was innocent and unfortunate, coming across the naked Goddess merely by chance.

Visual representation of the hunter's transformation has proved tricky. Titian worked on *The Death of Actaeon* from approximately 1559 and it remained unfinished in his studio at his death. Seeing this painting recently alongside *Diana and Actaeon* in the National Gallery of Scotland, its fluid, agitated surface, where bark is akin to flesh, foam on water indistinguishable from sunlight on petals, seems the best way to convey the agony of Actaeon's metamorphosis. A deer's head springs from between his shoulders, but the antlers are small, maybe to emphasise his youth, and the eye, looking wildly around, is recognisable as the one expressing surprise in the earlier picture. His hands and feet are reconfiguring into split hooves, and what looks like the remains of his trousers, melding into the mouths and limbs of the dogs who are overwhelming him, could just as easily be the deer's pelt.

Other pictures try, less successfully, to find a moment that encapsulates both what Actaeon has been and what he is about to become. So it is usually an ungainly, elaborately-antlered biped that the hounds tear apart, still clothed and maybe even grasping a weapon in one of his hands. It's hard to imagine such a creature marvelling at the speed of which he suddenly finds himself capable. In Ovid's text, Actaeon's mind is the only part of him which remains human. Before he lowers his head to drink at another forest pool and is confronted with the reflection of the stag he has become, he has no idea what has happened to him. 'And down the eyes that were not his his bitter tears did rain.' (Bk 3, line 240)

Lucas Cranach the Elder's *Diana und Aktaon* (*c.*1518) telescopes the two crisis points of the story into one. As Diana splashes water in Actaeon's face, the drops rising from her hand double as the tears springing from his eyes. He is sitting at the edge of the pool, all transformed apart from his legs, which are encased in black hose. The tawny covering of his trunk could be either stag's hide or a hunter's deerskin jerkin. His arms have become the stag's front legs, but as he is sitting down, he waves them in the air with a recognisably human gesture, simultaneously protesting and trying to protect himself against the dogs already attacking him. Other deer, pursued by hounds, and a huntsman with horn, are visible in the background.

In Ovid's text, the hounds tear Actaeon apart even as his huntsmen are calling him to come and take his part in the slaughter of this unexpected prize. He dies with his own name echoing in his ears; that every attempt to answer is heard as another bellow from the wounded stag adds to the melancholy of the scene. By naming and characterising these hounds as individuals, Ovid shares with the reader the kind of knowledge only someone, like Actaeon, who spent so much of his time with them would have had. Golding translates literally the names that seem natural in English and adapts others to make them so in a way that conveys all the excitement and exertion of the chase and the terrible violence of its ending: Blackfoot, Stalker, Spy, Eatall, Scalecliff, Killbuck, Savage, Spring, Hunter, Lightfoot, Woodman, Shepherd, Laund, Greedygut, Ladon, Blab, Fleetwood, Patch, Wight, Bowman, Roister, Beauty, Tawny, Ruffler, Tempest, Coal, Swift, Wolf, Snatch, Rug, Jollyboy, Churl, Ringwood, Slow, Killdeer, Hillbred.

The feeling that the hounds are varied, individual characters rather than cells in an anonymous pack may have fed into the interpretation of Actaeon's story developed in Giordano Bruno's *De gli eroici furori / The Heroic Frenzies* (1585). Here the hunter's fate is not explained as an unlucky

[105]

blunder followed by an act of disproportionate retribution. Instead Actaeon is presented as a seeker after truth. His dogs represent his thoughts; mastiffs stand for his will and greyhounds for the quickness and agility of his cognitive processes. Diana, in her character of the moon reflecting the sun's much brighter and completely unapproachable light, is the purest form of truth accessible on earth. Actaeon's fate, after gazing on her naked form, is to become what he has pursued and to be dragged down and consumed by his own thoughts. In Pieter van Harinxma's watercolour and ink drawing *Aktaion betrapt Artemis* (1628–30), the 'palmed horns' (Bk 3, line 162) Actaeon sprouts at the moment Diana becomes aware he has discovered her are mirrored by the recumbent crescent moon balancing on the goddess's head. The left arms of both are extended in a nearly identical gesture. Diana points at Actaeon who, following her line across the picture, flings his arm out in surprise.

'Then the soul will proceed to traverse the forest of natural phenomena where so many objects are hidden under a shadow and cloak; for in a thick, dense and deserted solitude the truth voluntarily seeks cavernous retreats, interwoven with thickets and surrounded by wooden, rugged and leafy plants, and there for the most worthy and excellent reasons she conceals, veils and buries herself with the greatest vigilance . . .

'Therefore truth is sought as something inaccessible, an object beyond objectivity and beyond all comprehension. For that reason it is impossible for anyone to see the sun, the universal Apollo and absolute light as the supreme and most excellent species; but very possible to see its shadow, its Diana, the world, the universe, the nature which is in things, the light shining through the obscurity of matter and so resplendent in the darkness . . .

'I say very few are the Actaeons to whom destiny gives the power to contemplate Diana naked, and the power to become so enamoured of the beautiful harmony of the body of nature, so fallen beneath the gaze of those two lights of the dual splendor of goodness and beauty, that they are transformed into deer, inasmuch as they are no longer the hunters but the hunted . . .

'*Ecce elongavi fugiens, et mansi in solitudine.* [Lo, I have gone far off flying away; and I abode in the wilderness. (Psalms 54.8)]'

from Giordano Bruno's *The Heroic Frenzies; part 2, 2nd Dialogue.*

Thomas Wright, *Isaac Watts and Contemporary Hymn-Writers*, 1914 [p.192]

Isaac Watts, *A Funeral Poem on Thomas Gunston Esq.*, 1701 [lines 63–66]

All quotations from Ovid *Metamorphoses* Book 3 are taken from Arthur Golding's translation (1567) edited by Madeleine Forey, Penguin, 2002 [pp.98–102]

Erasmus Darwin, *Loves of the Plants* (Bk 2 of *The Botanic Garden*) 1791 [preface]

George Collison, *Cemetery Interment*, 1840 [p.230]

Rev. John Stoughton, *Shades and Echoes of Old London*, 1864 [p.89]

Edward Walford, *Old and New London*, 1878 [vol. 5, chapters 43–44]

Anna Maria Fielding (Mrs S. C.) Hall, *Pilgrimages to English Shrines*, 1854 [p.233]

Francis Bacon, *On Gardens*, 1625

Paul Joyce, *A Guide to Abney Park Cemetery*, 2nd edition, 1994

Giordano Bruno, *De gli eroici furori / The Heroic Frenzies*; Second Part, Second Dialogue (1585) translated by Paul Eugene Memmo, Chapel Hill, University of North Carolina Press, 1966 [pp.223–225]

'The Hunter' comes from an ongoing project looking at how people record their experience of a place and the narratives they may make about it. It is loosely centred round Abney Park Cemetery in north London. Other texts can be read online at www.3ammagazine.com

YOLSKI

Drawings

Brittany Landscape, 1994, black chalk on white paper, 152 x 112 mm

Departure, 1998, black chalk drawing on white paper, 100 x 90 mm

Winter Travel with Walnuts, 1998, black chalk drawing on white paper, 150 x 90 mm

Wintertime Reading at Home, 2001, pen and black ink on white paper, 74 x 211 mm

Winter Evening, 1998, black chalk drawing on white paper, 49 x 271 mm

Sketch from Waiting series, 2003, pen and black ink on ivory paper, 93 x 139 mm

JØRN H SVÆREN

translated from the Norwegian by the Author

INSERT

It is Thursday morning the 5th of September 2013, I am standing by the window next to the balcony on the first floor of the old dairy at Blaker. In the window frame before me, leaning against the windowpane, are three rizas which have arrived with the mail from an auction house in Århus. The word riza is Russian and designates a metal cover protecting an icon. An icon is an image of a saint in the Orthodox Church. A riza covers the whole image with the exception of the heads, hands and feet of the holy. It lays bare the skin and conceals everything else. It is strange, I have seen images of saints where the surface of the painting is almost empty, only heads and hands are depicted. They float in the thin air. They are made to be covered up. A riza is often made of a precious metal, it shall both honour the image and protect it, from soot and dirt and touch. The believers light candles before the images and they kiss them and run their fingers over them. The images hang in icon corners in homes and in churches at designated places. Christ is enthroned to the right of the Royal Doors, the double doors at the centre of the iconostasis, the image wall separating the nave from the sanctuary, the congregation from the clergy, in an Orthodox church. The Mother of God, Madonna with the Child, is depicted on the opposite side. The Royal Doors lead to the altar, they are closed to the congregation, which can only see into the sanctuary when the doors are opened at certain points in the liturgy. I am standing looking at the three rizas in the window frame before me, they conceal nothing, there are no images behind them, the holes in the metal covers radiate with daylight. Yet I can envisage the images, I recognize

the outlines, the stylized figures, recurring in the art of the Orthodox
Church: two heads, one leaning towards the other—it is the Virgin again,
with her son in her lap, she bends her head towards him and he looks
at us and lifts his hand to heaven. I remember another figure, a strongly
simplified story, from a stone church on a mountain ridge in the north-
west of Spain, on the border between Galicia and Castilla y León. The
moss-grey building lies behind a wall against the road, I went over to
the low door at the foot of the bell tower and pushed it open. I went in
and looked around me, the room was small and austere, with wooden
benches and whitewashed stone walls. On the side walls, at regular inter-
vals, hung fourteen simple wooden crosses. They symbolize the Way of
the Cross, the Way of Suffering, the fourteen stations of the Passion of
Christ, from when he is condemned to death till he dies on the cross and
is taken down and laid in the tomb. The fourteen scenes are portrayed
in most Catholic churches, as paintings, memorial tablets or sculptures
along the walls. I have seen frescoes from floor to ceiling and marble
groups the size of men, irreplaceable. Here, on the other hand, in this
rural church, high up under heaven, simplicity reigned. The fourteen
crosses looked the same, nothing distinguished them from each other, no
Roman numerals carved into the woodwork, nothing. I have never seen
a simpler depiction of the Way. The radical simplification speaks of a
common, deeply rooted imagery, people knew the Passion, they carried
it with them, fourteen wooden crosses were enough to evoke the series
of images in the mind. I stand before the first cross and see Jesus being
condemned to death. I stand before the second and see Jesus taking up
the cross. I stand before the third and see Jesus falling for the first time
beneath the cross. And so on, from cross to cross throughout the room.
I go anticlockwise, in accordance with tradition, from the north side,
the Gospel side of the altar. I think fourteen empty niches in the walls
would have evoked the same images, and I would have been uncertain
if there were fewer or more. I stop at the repetition and I recognize the

number. I have another memory from this borderland, from a room at a guest house behind the Benedictine monastery in the mountain village of Samos. A day has passed, it is early afternoon, my father stands unsettled in the bathroom door and asks me if I can cut his toenails. I am old and stiff, I cannot reach down, he says. I say yes and he gives me the scissors and sits down on the bed. I sit on the floor. I put his feet in my lap and we fall silent. I am grateful for this memory. I went to work carefully, I remember the uneasiness and the intimacy and the concentration on the task, the soft resistance of the nails and the dry clicks when they gave in. I remember the silence that followed and the bells that chimed for vespers, I went to the church along the massive stone walls, the monastery in Samos is among the largest in the Western world. I went in and sat down and waited. I thought about the small things, and the last things, all this to come. A young novice lights the candles. The monks gather, dressed in black and bent with age, they sing with cracked voices. So it shall always be. I closed my eyes and asked for time.

———

for Guttorm Guttormsgaard's Archive, June 2014

The Norwegian original first published as a loose-leaf insert to the chapbook *Vi er tiggere* [*We Are Beggars*] (Oslo, England Forlag, 2014)
riza, unknown artist, Russia, *c.*1800–1899, brass
depicted here from the back, 259 x 318 x 22 mm
photo courtesy Silje Schild / The Guttormsgaard Archive 2014
http://guttormsgaardsarkiv.no

ERIKA DAGNINO

translated from the Italian by the Author with

EMILIA TELESE

from

CANTI OF THE EYE

I

The gaze warring between itself and its blood divides into rain, of
fragments, perhaps saline, perhaps of fog.
Humidity is separated, under the leafy shiny regurgitation,
so it is accompanied by the harsh burning of a broken trunk.
In jolts breath seeks oxygen in the most perceptible layers of
atmospheric brevity.
With our parallel shadows, distanced to comprehend one singular
way.
Under the closed lids a single veil of light is disclosed.
It is the gusts failing to prevent the shadow from touching you,
from the leaves to you every shape shakes and escapes with all the
tragic gentleness of velocity.
The plant has a voice when it speaks and when it is quiet, its voice
is the raw aroma of the branch, or flower, or foliage.
The pulsations do not allow scraping as if under our steps the
asphalt is overwhelmed by the spasm of autumn. Your breath shores
up the pouring gesture of what is subtraction or communion.
To gaze upon you as one gazes upon death.
Your salty voice is amongst the shimmer, where the imminent wave
breathes you.

II

From the implacable frame of the sky, the disclosure of an
exception to joy is about to hurl down as an exception to the
discernment of truth.
The convoluted step gives way under the mute intrusiveness of the
branch, where the verbose roots emerge from the earth eradicated
from the soil by the elusive shaking,
such as comes from the grey of the sky.
It dies under flexible, dies under audible, under dying mucilages
escaped backwards by the uninhabitable. Disguised as ardent
movement and yet freezing, foliage.
Thus under the kiss your brow
has turned icy, for a wind that only in the air leaves no trace.
In the false moonlight the foam lies in its own convulsions, coming
from an even more obscure diaphragm. Which opens like a cut
under the foot, to dirty clotted sweat.
On reaching it dies, on reaching it dies; on reaching
it dies, here is a faint passage, immune to each
impervious part of direction.

III

We can slumber like the flower that pretends to flower,
or reduce reality by beginning to strip the nail from our point of
departure, which our heart stares at as if it were juice, as if it were
thirst.
Then the sky in beating each remaining segment, escaped from our
mouths, its rain, its rain, fall of hammers elusively viscous.
Rusty pulp, each fragment of rain.

Uningestible pulp for every morsel of ours, or lip, or kiss.
The whisper has not made its way, among all these sounds fallen in
a heap, thus fallen again towards the sky, it has lost its whispering
structure. Or rather its structure has held on, in order to rise in all
its insufficient shadow.
It is through starting from exceptions that it all makes sense. In
going around partitions and partings, each circle would then
pulsate under the pallor of a single dual skin.

IV

Upon the suture that falsely unites sky and sea, where from afar
where inside the eye of bruise, and it becomes rippled, heave the
nailed thistles to the breath,
theirs are the hollow shapes of webs ripped from themselves, from
the absence of a perpetual silence.
The groove of thorns seemingly to divide the wave, each groove
floats, a drift of sweetish, rusty, woody sounds, as the constricted
gestures of the dead move away.
We have only our exiled fingers to defend the eyes from the
disconnected quiver of the dew, which becomes salty like dew like
uncertain dew. As our sole support to repair the vitreous.
The gleam of the curve pushed by the taut fishbone stays hidden,
colourless from the hindrance of the gaze; even fish can be
underground, only to skin itself leap after after leap under the
sandy wavy movement. Each grain mixed with water amounts to
mud, it turns to foam, turns to mud, to be reached by the chaotic
groove.

V

It splits behind you the sound of two grinding stones, flint the
one and the other,
it splits and at the back of your back I see and look and I upset the
limit of the vitreous humour.
Eyeless, from sound to sound glitters the lack of ground. Reduced
to disembowelled earth; to fallen trunks; there are geometries
occupying the space, others that suffocate it while occupying it.
Walls are missing, reduced to a slender cluster of autumnal shrub,
the hand can contain it so that each berry unripe or red
covers lines of the route, not before the abandonment of splinters
on the ground on the fall with broken sound.
For each wrinkled up berry, a dull pulpitation abandons to its fate
any trace of heartbeat.

VI

Resins offer, beyond each footprint of ours, a vague scent of
mortality. Trusting their fate of bark, their piece of torn trunk, on
the ground like prematurely fallen crust, in time to reveal a sort of
unbreathable infection.
It's in the back of my eye that you drink my kiss, its very water
leads the vision, its inborn transparency; to your gesture I leave a
kind of collision; it brings with it, especially to white, a change of
chromatic nuances.
It is not time that makes changes. We mutate to the thrusts of our
directions.
From shadow to shadow you lie at the back of my gaze, breath does
not divide to cloud the vision, when it blurs it discloses access to
the different reality. Outside of us it may be night, or maybe day;
it's at the back of the eyes that we overcome this regular alternation.

VII

To support ourselves on the irregular path, we grasp the persistence
of the branch.
It's this dampness of tears emerging from the groove of our palms.
Not even hesitation wakes us in front of the heavy trunk, hewn with
the aid of bad weather.
From our gesture a little blood gushes out warning us of the
consistence of our echoes. It's the ankles balancing between one bark
and the other, the ankles to surveillance and survey,
as if between the wind and the sea the only way were an open trap.
Nostalgia is to exile as incompleteness is to immortality.
We wait looking through the darkness for the passage of a black
meteor. We wait looking through the darkness for the black of every
dark passage. The cold saves us the visible toil of the ants' nest.
The purity of any animal eye, remote to the ghost of any dissonance.

Your lips cut the foliage, almost as if your own mouth chewed it.
Next to our space an air with the aspect of night strikes wood
and decay. Yet the rain has the same hardness as stone or sharp or
ground. If we look at the luminous half of a circle, in our spot the
puddle takes on time. If we look at the shadow, then each body takes
on its distance. I try to touch you as if you were of lake and of lake
and of lips, I stop before each scrupulous calcification, for the breath
meeting with the cold. Each quiver lies on the ground supine, just
slightly stretched out like the eye of each snail;
if recoiling, where it recoils, it recoils,
turning only into body.

Until the air overflows, let us hurl them down one by one our
winged insects. Those fallen while sleeping, fallen on a mortal
slumber; but those mindful of flight, fail not to teach themselves
through the sky's bruises. Each rustle of wings a bluish rustle, each
rustle of wings to sanction the appearance of the collision.
The eyes stagger yet to be terrified.
But no, we do not owe anything we do not possess; we wander
around our openings by our very nature. If I kiss you I take my lips
to kiss your brow, to touch how thinness and your blood magnify
under the skin. Any moment now, no, we have never stopped
listening to the pride of every fall, the viscosity of the air, the
humming of the wake.

X

Cold moves to the centre of the trunk; if fallen, in the centre.
Where shadow in shatters becomes bark.
The gaze while looking clashes against everything: branches,
glimpses, eyes; the changing of directions, of green, of fingers. Fog
is an optical tunnel, corridor to our visions, penetrating it dilates us
and penetrates us, assisting the tenacity of our pupils, of our irises,
of the white. Repeatedly the gaze clashes, now it is our eyes that are
involved, almost as if they implied a sort of vague hostility, ready
to break bark and shadow and shadows and bark and underneath
and inside us.
Desperation comes between us like a thin bridge, ferrying us over
the abyss, our bodies and us.
From digression to decay, from the weight of the body the fall
makes space, it chooses the direction falling as one falls asleep.

DUCK BAKER

STRAWBERRY BLONDE

"Strawberry Blonde" is one of some 70 pieces composed as part of a commission from Luigi Maramotti during 2013–2014. Most of these pieces are jazz tunes arranged for fingerstyle guitar, and this one is no exception, though by omitting the first A and B sections on the repeat it could be played straight, with no improvisation. The title owes to the melodic similarity in the first two measures to the well known 1895 hit popular song by John F. Palmer, "The Band Played On." The words to the verse of this charming period piece are worth remembering:

Casey would waltz with a strawberry blonde
And the band played on;
He'd glide 'cross the floor with the girl he adored
And the band played on;
But his brain was so loaded it nearly exploded
The poor girl would shake with alarm;
He'd ne'er leave the girl with the strawberry curls
And the band played on.

Strawberry Blonde

Duck Baker

4

D.C. al Coda

On the repeat, A1, B, and A2 are improv over chord seqence, returning to score at C

fin

PIERRE REVERDY

translated from the French by

BARRY SCHWABSKY

Five Poems

Secret

Vacant bell
Dead birds
In the house where everything's nodded off
Nine o'clock

Earth holds itself motionless
                You would say that someone was sighing
The trees wear the ghost of a smile
                Water trembles at the tip of each leaf
                A cloud crosses the sky

Outside the door a man is singing

                The window opens without a sound

WORD COMES DOWN

All the poppy flowers or women's lips
       reflected in the sky
It's rained
Kids drowning on sidewalks
And the street's tide
The city as funnel

In profile the day slips toward sunset
The cobblestone comes loose
And the tim'rous beasties
   at the wind's racket
       skedaddle
          And their names are

On the balconies the windowpanes tremble
       —just a moment—
The house is feverish
5 o'clock
Except the night that gets mixed up with the twisting
The trees at prayer

WAR

Earth immobilized
And the burning summer
Careful
Your protective helmet
I'm suited up
and the coming winter
forget it
We doubt ourselves all the more
You can try not to think so
Handkerchiefs hanging from balconies
        as flags of celebration
their colors washed out
And the distraught figure
Face of faces
Death saunters down the road
waiting for each of us to bow
But what other weight than your body's
        have you thrown on the scale
So cold in the trench
He sleeps with no more dreams

PREWAR PLEASURES

A thirsty head
And there's that moment when every leaf shivers
Lit cigars behind a plank wall
      where the legs vanish
      Gloved fingers in the bouquet
      Leaves
        They've wrecked everything
There's still a date pinned to the wall
      Some wandering musicians left there
      Birds mimic the musicians
        Soldiers mimic the birds
The biggest one bends over before leaving
        before falling
   The pointed wings are finally lifted up
Speed rubbed out each body along the path
      And the pacified river
Then the road down opened out
Cut into slices the sunbeam hides away its pearls
And we went bit by bit
      as far as the last plane tree
Toward open sky
      to stretch out at last
Against the wind that won't pass

Closed Frames

The light remains undecided
Briefly hesitates before each door in turn
And its sorrow clarifies
Beneath the palm tree that's been brought in

It's the joy of children's cries
Words that balance out
In your heart when it's stripped
Of feelings long since grown burdensome

A voice went offstage singing
Into the blue wings of the evening
That time the day was running late
And your sky so bright

Over these roads to your childhood
Where you ran with bare head and heart
What faces could you make out
In your memory the silence

———

Pierre Reverdy, Œuvres complètes, ed. Étienne-Alain Hubert
2 vols (Paris, Flammarion, 2010)

JOHN SEED

from

BRANDON PITHOUSE: RECOLLECTIONS
OF THE DURHAM COALFIELD

3

Dick Morris

It was the custom among miners for them

to take their sons with them

in the school holidays

and I was down

Oh I should think

a dozen times

with me dad

in the school holidays

just to see

was to get you acclimatised

the inevitable way of life

—

William Cowburn

You knew

long before you left school

that's where you were going when you left school that was

what you were

born for really to go down the pit

I should never been a pitman

in them days like

lots of liked the thought of going down

them getting a pony to drive

bit of attraction

but then I'm not frightened to admit

I was terrified when I went down the pit

I think I cried all the first shift

place was infested with rats

used to come out in swarms

come right to your feet

after the ponies' corn

—

I asked to go into the pit

to get away from school

I would go to school now

if I could be allowed

—

In the summer we go down at five.

In winter at three and up between three and four.

We come up in summer two or three in the afternoon.

Summer time when the work is not hard after the pit we play marbles

touching one another and try to catch quoits and cricket and striking a

ball against the wall.

Some boys go and fish eels in the river.

In winter time the hours are harder and when we come home we are fit

enough to go to bed.

—

I left school Monday

started work down the pit

Tuesday I was 14

pushing empty tubs on to

a creeper and I hated

it and hated all the

time I worked there for

six years I worked there

and hated it every minute

of it I developed more

muscles than what I thought

I had and very little

money

joy came the day

I left to join the

army goodbye to Wingate pit

—

Out-bye on the engine plane

middle of the way round a curve

the hauling engineman put his brake on

suddenly

the tail rope jerked and

flew off the binding sheaves across

into the middle of the way and

caught him on the head

fracturing his skull

—

15 hours out of the house every day I go to school at night   we are in school

two hours   I hurt myself very sore to get scholarship   I am ciphering and

am at squaring dimensions   I read well   I sometimes read the History of

England   sometimes I read the Bible   I write I cannot say very well but

I can write

—

5

inland shores in the pit   what the wavy floor was

and blue stone soft like when we were kids we used to write with at school

when it got wet it buried you like the houses on the Isle of White are sliding into

       the sea

in this band of stone are the fossils of the dinosaur we called it blos stone or mall

—

Nigh-hand gannen

parallel passages called boards

four yards wide eight yards asunder

connected by headways

smaller passages at right angles twenty yards apart

leaving strong pillars of coal to support the roof

headways and boards at right lines through the whole extent of the mine

seams of coal generally extend a great way

rising or falling or horizontal

workings branch out from one another

an immense number of dark passages

—

Durham a dense tropical rainforest wide rivers flowing to the sea
flooding left thick layers of sand and mud on top of vegetable matter decom-
posed and compressed

in low-lying swamps peat then new layers of peat

process repeated over millions of years layer after layer of mudstone sandstone
strata sequence of Westphalian coal measures bands of shale

steam coal house coal chinley coal gas coal claggy coal manufacturing coal sea
coal bunker coal pan coal crow coal sooty coal roondy coal coking coal cannel
coal brown coal shaly coal parrot coal beany coal

—

Old workings and air-ways where nobody was working so quiet you could hear
your own heart beating in the strata the forms of a leaf or a fish in the stone the
iron quartz pyrites sparkling like gold

—

The roadway was 14 feet high

held up with arched girders

coalface around 30 inches high

but with 4 inches of steel top and bottom

you had 22 inches to crawl through

some coalfaces were 6 miles out

—

Brian Muter

Well   you always   you had either a pricker or a stick and you used to tap

the top just to check   what the condition   the stone   was like   if it

was   you used to get a nice ring if it was alright   if it was   you used

to get like a holla sound if conditions were poor and you'd shove props in as

soon as you possibly could if you had the holla sound

—

PHILIPPE JACCOTTET

translated from the French by

IAN BRINTON

CONCERNING *Le Grand Recueil*

Should it ever cross the river's mind to scorn the rock for its unmoving density it would be more than likely that the rock in turn would consider the river too evasive with its quick and darting movement. That notwithstanding and, knowing myself with a certain degree of shame and irritation to be both inconsistent and "adaptable", I am particularly sensitive to certain weighty and specific words, certain blocks of language marked by a distinct air of unrefinement: in the real sense of that word. In this respect, and despite all obvious differences, I have for a long time linked together in my mind the names of Ramuz, Claudel and Ponge thinking that I'm fully aware of what that link is: a certain liking for objects placed side-by-side with a certain misgiving concerning abstract ideas (convincing parallels will I am sure be easily found in everyone's thoughts). The imagery of those writers carries a weighty physical presence of the perceived object; it's in their vocabulary and, above all, in the measured tread of their sentences; in particular it is to be found in everything about them that does not consist of glimmerings, light shafts, movements of breath, those inconsistencies within which I myself feel closely webbed. Pebbles, walls of vines, rocks, mountains; the pigs and cattle; domestic tools: these appear before my eyes and without stretching it too far I can recognise the precision of the writing. Now let's cut to the chase: it seems to me that each of these three poets has, in his own individual way, discovered a solid foundation to be located within the hurly-burly of spectres which for Ponge makes up our world.

*

However, I want now to leave behind those other two names who introduced me to Francis Ponge about fifteen years ago in order to enter the realm of his work itself and discover other even more remarkable reasons for both admiring and liking him. I shall sketch out a list of delights:

Grasses: clouds of green, always looking cool (1927).
The cloud: a block of feathery droplets (1938).
Prawns: a wary monster, a bright shining confusion (1926–1934).
Mistletoe: a northern mimosa, one suited to foggy climes (1941).
Anthracite: the power to burn for a long time buried in subsoil (1941).
The horse: foam at the lips, feather plume at the rear and key in the lock of the nostril (1948–1951).
The stone of an apricot: like a sun in eclipse seen through a smoky glass it throws out fire and flames.
The flower: the flower is an angel with pointed wings, harbinger of future roundness: the fruit (1960).

Perhaps there haven't been such images in poetry since Gongora; or perhaps I should say, such images of this type: "a block of feathery droplets" where the crystal and the feather are among those highlights of the expansive magical light of Cordoba. And also that other startling attempt to capture an aspect of the prawn in "bright shining confusion".

These images, from Spain and from Nîmes, certainly bring together in their audacity a boldness both of perception and of language which remains truly in focus without overdoing it (in which regard one might say that the arrow that hits the target has overstepped the mark). But to say the "kitten-headed dew" is that too surprising, too physical too much trying to be poetical? The daring of the surrealist seems to me like the blind man who doesn't see the dangers in front of him but for every hundred failures hits on a wonderful conceit by chance; and how many, following in the footsteps of some great and truly inspired visionaries, some Tiresias-like André Breton, have put a blindfold round their eyes on account of its being an effortless gesture to prevent them from seeing the pitfalls. And here I find an even greater sense of daring, one which is clear; a more fruitful sense of daring on account of its being focussed upon objective truthfulness rather than on itself; an audacious respect supported by powers of reason rather than defying them leading to the enlarging and enriching of those powers.

This audacity is accompanied naturally enough by light, flashes, speed of movement; even if the search is slow, patient, almost meticulous, one arrives all of a sudden at the "bright shining of confusion", which is to say at the meeting-point (complex, surprising but decisively clear) at which in two or four words seemingly contradictory ideas of fragility, solidity, a flash in the air, light versus darkness playfully mix together; physical and moral order merge together; and, even more, tones that are both high-pitched and muted are indissolubly bound together. One reaches this complex, these riches, this density of compression and control which is the distinguishing mark of the poet amid the general stammer. The fully justified boldness of these carefully devised images breathes fire into our minds and in response we begin to burn: we come alive. So it's no surprise to me that Francis Ponge, after exploring his aptitude for bringing life to clearly defined and static objects, should, over the past fifteen years, have developed his work to allow more aerial aspects of reality to become the subject of debate: swallows, electricity, horses, the glowing sheen of both apricots and sunshine.

☆

These images transfer ideas into poetry, sometimes bursting into flame before dying out but occasionally bringing them to ignition point at which they eclipse their surroundings; I have suggested that they "play" together and it is indeed an act of supreme wit that they perform in Ponge's work. They are jests in the sense of freedom from restriction, refusing to obey the laws of time, bowing down less and less to the world of theory; and they are jests in the way they move sometimes from impertinence to delight, from the mystery of a Chinese smile to a roar of Roman exultation; jests which doff their caps to reason in order to cut short outrageous flights of fancy. These writings are jests in the way they are governed by different combinations of clear rules leading to a good-humoured tone of confrontation between words and objects. However, we also note that this playfulness which has, ever since those years of *Parti pris des choses*, closely resembled a game of chess or solitaire has now in recent years become another indoor pursuit played on tables of wood and felt expanding into a merry-go-round as though by Fautrier rolled out in 1606 in the most spirited, magnificent and agile manner: all of which is to say that Francis Ponge no longer fights shy of a certain panache, a certain pomp, a grandeur and expansiveness; as well as a fast-moving rate, cocking a snook at death, degradation and stupidity. And so at length in an unforeseen and most touching manner these jests sometimes find a parallel with those one associates with the sacred as one can see cheerfully placed on Etruscan tombs or the serious and noble unfolding of frescoes near Pompei: in this manner, seemingly an ultra-modern long way round, we discover a certain pre-Christian depth as is fostered for instance in the brilliant text of "The Goat".

*

I think that it is worth highlighting these little thoughts here since nobody, as far as I am aware, has noted or emphasised the shift to which I am referring. Yet again it would be better if my notes should not bang on too much otherwise people will think that Ponge has turned backwards whereas he has actually been moving forwards guided by his own tastes and regaining his former grandeur.

At the end of the line, having walked through *Le Grand Recueil* without too many preconceptions or deliberate intentions (and yet without ceasing to admire the fact that there is no line in all three books that doesn't bear the hallmark of his individual genius) it seems to me that the primary thrust which is apparent is one of enthusiasm whilst the second thrust reveals a precision which acts as a brake. Or, to put it in his own style, it is fire that is tamed by wit. Watch him, with astonishment and belief, at work in "The Glass of Water" as he leads you on from a world of things to a world of words:

I am the tapper of a tumbler of water. I tap on the top like a tuner to get the right note in a manner that is tiresomely like a child when it has once found out how to do it.

In the work of Francis Ponge (and I refer here also to the man himself) there is a power of exceptional and highly individual concentration. This is not a mechanical attention to detail but an all-consuming focus on certain objects and it is above all both approving and glorifying, specifying details for the best of reasons and never in a silly way.

This twin movement of enthusiastic engagement and clarity of attention, a passionate attachment followed by an objective detachment, holds up these two worlds of objects and language reflecting the individuality of this writer. To my mind it is essential to insist that Ponge is never interested in language for its own sake. I see his achievement as being at its greatest in terms of the audacity and inventiveness revealed in the work produced over the last fifteen years.

*

To disqualify everything that has been said in such a densely philosophical way about his exceptional nature and also to put into perspective weaknesses in his own work (no one knowing the dangers of these more than the author himself) I quote for you with pleasure the page that he wrote on 22nd December 1947 in Sidi-Madani. I would rather extract a few lines to direct the reader back to the whole rich field of *Le Grand Recueil*, lines which are representative of the whole swirl of ideas located there:

I want all people reading my work to look at it on the same level; to feel themselves relaxed at its directness; to wander round it at ease recognising the familiar within the revelation; to take note of the evidence offered, the light, the temperature, the harmony.
Yet at the same time I want everything to be new, unexplored, a new dawn rising.
Plenty of ordinary words still lack usage and the most obvious have not yet been written.
This evening for a moment my little ouverture, a skylight in fact which
looks through an immense wall, is the picture-window in front of which we love to sit.

The garret window was like a lime lit up.
Is every lime like a window?
At twilight the sky ripens quickly . . . Limelight!

———

in Philippe Jaccottet, *L'Entretien des Muses: Chroniques de poésie* (Paris, Gallimard, 1968)

JASMINE JOHNSON

SAVAGE TOURISM [E-READER EDITION]

both: black ink on paper, 297 x 420 mm, India, 2014

Tobias sat across from the TV presenter. Behind them a peace lily and a backdrop of a city by night, streetlights and lit-up windows formed grids. The presenter looked directly down the camera lens. 'Did they have a family structure as we know it? The cannibals?' 'No. No, nobody got married, they had a kind of free and open society.' Tobias cracked a smile. 'What can I say?' 'Like the hippies?' The woman next to Tobias cut in. The audience roared with laughter. 'No it wasn't like the hippies. They were for real these people.' The presenter tilted his head to the right. 'Did they still engage – you said – they still engage in cannibalism?' Tobias looked up: He raised his hand and waved it gently from left to right. 'Only in the en...' he closed his eyes 'upstream parts.' 'Where you were?' Tobias nodded. 'It did happen yes. But rarely.' 'What are you gonna do when they did that?' The presenter said. 'Well they didn't eat me!' Tobias' eyes bulged 'But I mean, did you see it? Did

CAROLINE CLARK

Poems from the Heart

There's a spot outside
my house a widening in
the road where cars must
stop before moving on but
when empty of traffic early
morning it could reach
anywhere beyond this
moment of cessation.

Speak to me please
as if I were foreign.
I will not seek to
join your game for
I know not how.

To have it all again
the roses
the first star that appears
when the evening lays ahead
with its warm promise.

Time was when we
did not live fearlessly
but were fearless in
our belief that the way
would become apparent.

The day lengthens
the daffodil blooms
soon a March moon
to make you want more.

What was there? Churchbells
and a white magnolia starring into
the blue sky early May morning.
Let the bells ring until
I can answer.

Two arms flung back
asleep in this supple
backwards embrace.
She has known no
machine yet to put
her body askew. I
ache and crack
allow my shoulders
to drop. Youth says, here
this way you once knew.

Dear heart what
have you done to me?
We lived elevated to the dream.
We returned to find all was lost.

this crystalline joy
melting into
remembrance

There,
our lives
gleaming
glistening
in the setting sun
glinting with all
we have
left behind.

scent of first melt-
               water ozone heady
                               I'm as high as a ribbon of cloud stretching to Tallinn
         take me down
impossible

The bluebells
were beautiful
this year. We
would go back
to check on them.
Hope in all we
do then defeat.

Memorialise
touch the dust

the dust the sparrows
bathe in

the dust the *dvorniki*
sweep away.

Unattended grave
first day of the year
now visited.

YAMUPH PIKLÉ

Through Engagement
(An Intimate Moment, 3)

Weakest history distils the answer.
Aether surrounding the box can be
bypassed entirely, divides between
days
       load entirely still within aether.
Primary breakthrough mushroomed
completion, the field was a woman
's. Five years passed where the sun rose.
Seconds distracted from the main event,
marathon inauguration.
                   Super categorical.
From aether's vantage were sent construction
missives, surveyors readied & scaffolds stockpiled.
Super perfection at variable completions,
time in accordance with quantity sustains quality.
Next advance
              aether's precursors less mined,
time scooping backwards on joy callipers,
the date of creation of the span of decades
was celebrated as speed runs. Research
& development slipped the various maps
in ten years
            the interim steadies
for twenty seconds this steadying corrodes
and is galvanised. The fantasy existed
where it soon crumbled with speed

its perimeters necessarily stripped
and passage granted in invisible
steps, again, hard
                    labour redefined
and in exertion steadied.
                            Colour elemental
switches & feel: the essences
retained this quality in passage insert
weather now and shade. Quick scans
the deepest history entirely falsifiable and
evident as the dew sets on code. Hail to the
co-creator. Hail to branding's sense of continuity.
Is this the love we hoped would curve our lines if
alien speed achieved dominion of the heart's delay?
The slow exploration of agon is itself a kind of justice
now. The marathon of continual expansion bites
thinking swoops. Cultivate fear
                            at the dark world, anxiety in the
light, slow steps in the temple grounds, created
for delight as attitudes without wonder: new
possessions! lost in catastrophic instigation.
As if its own path can reveal its length at each point.
Occluded play ghosts each run through
meditation transforming the plastic stormtrooper gun
to a stick
            slow gainful feedback
forms.
            Rewards encoded enterprise. Abuse is rife.
Completion. Faster, re-read from beginning to here.
Therapeutic expansion: the sixth chakra is opening
& inflows the history of empire. Ignorance itself
has come to contain knowledge its ward.

                    The denizens of risible pleasure
dream of Parisian card sharks, roulette table spins
etched in prose: the epic that justifies now
                               changes
flooded with a harmless blue light, a tree providing
a fine spectacle, embracing its loss to the crisp of
complicit order, an ethics of streams & replacement
artifice
          transfers scan again, staple
& mourn. It is already known. The
medium is input, the small stone
in order unfolding to its own state
& the factory in Germany serving
as proxy for the shoals and the
steady sense of cadence now
absent: its complete shadow
stated the absence of the statue
behind its fulfilment in fire and
water, its product the discs from
the code sent by discs.
                   Splicing
clear order comes out, donuts. Donations to the empire
hardwired to its soil an ocean apart, connections anterior
to land rift, where some thoughts say sleeping we still seek.
Serfdom bounty hunters, the galaxy desires interiority.
Starch fantasy commands empyrean in rift
networks quivered: multipliers boost
threads across his blazing tirade
in combinations of completion and notoriety
to the bath tub equipped with
Nicene scales handed down embossed with prayer
thought now in impulse with its own charm

hard arc to descend through two false entrances
conjoined.
          Crystal merchants start to see
increased change. With no desire for
transparency their base goods' accumulated
stains stop harming sense.
                  Possession slides with
culpability around a spiral definition, the camera
timed to catch each second pouring new miracle
canvases from the dark room. Historic calm remains
fantasy. Images
          strain complexion's
inches flat as imaginary sea.
             The dreams of seals came
with the first mentioned second,
             stretched
to accommodate the lyre's strings.
             Their
scroll paintings each unfold a plan for the
instrument. Small violence
       strum
       strum
       strum
so it wished to be ancient technique
& with the hacks was granted form
identical to such techniques. Risen
unchanged
encrypted deeper in the
vaults wish its tracks to curve in
to the mysteries. A final calming
knock
knock

knock
      floodlit gains. Shame pulses shade
chrysalides. Redemption flourishes
          struggle
          struggle
          struggle
lapping at ponds. The symbiote first to break
out from its jars attached to the core of the
serial tone. It drifted with time to this water,
prime to maintain its own vessel. In place its
history accrued new dimensions, building
itself upon postulated unknowns that twisted
into the complexities of its structure. Like
pinball it came to its own discoveries. By chance
it was granted its own brand of pinball machine

LEISURE APPEALS

Synthetic marsh. Become a special law decreed
Only audience initiate pleasure ground seem
For narrowness behind the façade of tranquil
Fingers. More taking back vases down stairs.
The hand movements of the jealous lover
Capacity far side of ice sunny on
Arrangement part of a face in profound repose
As is setting to a bachelor's carton while sleep
Transmits controversial doctrines into which
Buckle loan talent and others playing
Roots, line, everything. It led to nothing;

Nothing but a view at the end used to play
The natural limit and bulwark walking their rounds
To express in one word where flowers should be of
A moment abstract. Warm light, black gowns,
I firmly believe my joys & desires
Process by the same indulged clam mental
Preoccupation out lived this golden rule of
Vacation. Of this siege so badly turned if
These even are bronze bells. Sought in vain to destroy
Acquired steeper form rose placed and sheltered
English verdure, English culture, English comfort

Seen under a sun bright, without being oppressive
Free observation from discoursed and ground at
Escape. Course with mint and chaser few models
These borrowed images at loading what is life
Then walk but some seemed to need idiots boast
Of pageantry filter where out a way prized
Some are gone to the ponds rapid with handsome curves
Gone now. Paranoia optioned as to left
Optioned sentence hedge and fortune coning grasp
Desperate model or lighter kernel refreshing
Trouble and distress determined to go direct.

———

"Through Engagement (An Intimate Moment, 3)" belongs to section III
of *Conversations Heard Over Droning Sirens at the Yacht Marina*, a sequence
"Leisure Appeals" is a separate poem

CATULLUS

translated from the Latin by

SIMON SMITH

Seven Poems

5

Let's *really* live, Lesbia, which is to love,
and tote up the rumours and grumblings of grey,
old men, to be worth nothing but one sous.
Suns will set and suns will rise forever more,
for us, finally, our short life snuffed out,
one night, infinite, to sleep the big sleep.
Give me a thousand kisses, then one hundred,
then a thousand, then a second hundred more,
a thousand without a break, and a hundred—
then, when we're totaled up thousands on thousands,
we'll throw them in the air to lose the knowledge,
so no bad person control us with knowing
the grand equation of the sum of our kisses.

7

Your question, the total count of your kisses,
Lesbia, to satiate me, and the rest:
as many as there are Libyan sands out
there in lasarpicium-rich Cyrene,
reaching from the sweltering oracle of
Jupiter to the divine grave of Battus;
or as counted a multitude across night's
soundless stars overseeing secret lovemaking.
That's the sum of kisses kissed on kisses kissed.
These would more than satiate insane Catullus:
too numerous for busybodies to add up,
or the wicked spread vile rumours about.

Furius, you possess no slave or wallet,
not an arachnid, insect, or firewood,
but a father *and* a stepmother are yours
with gnashers hard enough to devour flint-stone.
What a wonderful life you spend with father
and the old fella's dried stick of a woman.
No surprise there—a happy family in
rude health, settled tummies without a care in
the World, no fires, no dilapidated homes,
no domestic violence or poisoning,
or other dangerous possibilities.
In any case, your bodies dry as old bones,
or drier even than that, if such a thing
exists, with freezing cold, sunshine, dieting.
So how come you're not so fit and well-off?
You've never broken into a sweat or drooled,
no gobbing, no sneezing, you've kept you're nose clean.
Now that's clean, clean, clean, and what's cleaner than clean,
an arsehole more polished than a saltcellar;
you can't be taking a dump more than ten times
a year, dessicated as beans, dry as stone,
if you squeezed it between the palms of your hands
you wouldn't force dirt under your fingernails.
These are fine endowments indeed, Furius,
neglect them not, nor disown these great riches,
and desist pursuing me for the hundred
thousand, as you're doing absolutely fine.

42

Come along, hendecasyllables, everyone
of you out of everywhere and every last one.
A cheeky scrubber has taken me for a ride
saying, if you don't mind, she'd rather not hand back
our notebooks—that's more than difficult to swallow.
We need to pursue her, require she give them up.
You may well ask which one is she? It's that one there
with the inelegant gait and histrionic
cackle, and all the looks of a real French bitch.
So, form a circle now, let's shout together,
'disgusting hooker hand over the notebooks now,
hand over the notebooks, you disgusting hooker.'
She flips us the 'v's. Ah, the scrubber, the hooker,
or whatever other name-calling you can think of.
But we cannot think the game's over with that.
We can do nothing more I suppose than make her
burn red in the face with complete embarrassment.
Yell at the top of your voices, all together:
'disgusting hooker hand over the notebooks now!
hand over the notebooks, you disgusting hooker!'
This is getting us nowhere, she doesn't bat an eyelid.
We'll have to adjust our pitch and methodology.
Let's give this a go and see where it might get us:
'Lady of Honour and Purity, my notebooks?'

55

We implore you, if it's not over-taxing,
reveal to me your darkest whereabouts.
I've been looking here and there in the Campus
Minor, the Circus Maximus, at the sign
of booksellers, the most sacred place of Jove.
I took a stroll down the Great Walk as well
my friend, quizzed every little tart there,
but they blinked back innocently enough.
'Turn him in,' I insisted of each one,
'give me Camerius, you sinful lot.'
'Right here,' called one, unlacing her thin slip,
'look here, he's resting between my rosy tits!'
All of this trouble you've been is the work
of Hercules, you're too snobby, compadre.
So, let us fix a venue and time, declare
it, commit to it, believe in daylight.
Do the pretty little blondes tether you down?
If you bite your tongue, remain tight-lipped
you'll have frittered away love's harvest.
Venus thrives on the fullness of rhetoric.
In any case, as you like it, zip it,
just as long as I'm cut my cut of your love.

63

Across deepest oceans Attis catapulted in his quick yacht,
headlong inland with flight of foot, to approach the Phrygian woods,
pressing forward and through dark woods, the goddess's crowning thicket,
and at that point tortured beyond sense, reason blinded beyond logic,
arrowhead razor-sharpened he sliced away his genitals.
So then *she* sensed her limbs useless, severed, lacking his manliness,
even as new blood spattered down, reddening the earth all around—
with the quickest of reactions, white-knuckled she shook the timbrel—
your timbrel, Cybebe, all yours, Matriarch—mysteries on high,
rattling and tapping out deftly, finger-tipped the sonorous hide,
and forthwith she started to sing, a-tremble, to her disciples:

'Up, up and away together, Gallae, to Cybele's tree-tops,
follow me together, lost of Dindymenian Domina,
who were quickly banished from homes, look towards foreign places,
tow my line of reasoning, accomplices on my pathway
have resisted sea currents and the fury of the oceans,
unmanning your own bodies, beyond total disgust for Love:
make ecstatic your goddess' heart with non-stop frenzied dancing.
Expunge all thought of postponement—all together, in my footsteps
to Phrygia, Cybele's home, to the goddess' Phrygian woods—
where voices of cymbals sing out, where tambourines echo reply,
where the Phrygian flautist booms deeper sounds from a curved horn,
where the Maenads garbed with ivy shake their heads in complete frenzy,
where with piercing cries blurted loud and clear they play out sacred rites,
where wayward followers to the goddess often fled on foot,
towards that place we must trip quick-stepping our way speedily.'

In that moment, no real woman, Attis sang to the company,
the whole troupe cried a-trembling, voices out loud ululating,
where tambourines rattled once more, again cymbals tinkled away,
on jostling, flitting feet the chorus converged towards verdant Ida.
Delirous, wobbly, panting, senseless, breathing her one last breath,
supported by tambourine, Attis unthinking, pressed through dark woods,
(a cow undomesticated, throwing off the weight of harness),
for the Gallae keenly to track their leader from her footsteps.
Cybebe's shrine attained, an effeminate lassitude fell
across them, sleepy after strife, huge labour without sustenance:
over tired eyes sleepiness ebbs and flows, enveloping eyes shut,
soothing frantic thoughts with quiet to melt desperation away.
But when the sun, bright, golden-faced, the piercing gaze of his warm eyes
scanned across the lucent sky, the harsh ground, the furious sea,
driving away shadowy night with his horses, a team fresh-shod,
then Sleep retreated quickly, (leaving Attis alert, wide awake),
to the Goddess Pasithea, enveloped in her pulsing heart.
So after quiet time and rest, free of over-heated panic,
when Attis reflected on those actions she herself had triggered
and saw in the cold light of day what she had come to, what was lost,
in chaotic and teeming thoughts she retraced her steps to the beach,
gazing over desolate seas, there she wept tears copiously,
in this pitiful state she spoke broken-voiced to her motherland:

'Oh my country which created me, oh my country where I was born
and pathetically abandoned, just as fugitive slaves abscond
their masters, and fled light-footed into Ida's dense woodland,
that I might live up in snowfields, amongst animals' frozen dens,
venturing in my distraction to seek their every habitat—
in what direction, whereabouts do I believe you are, my land?
My eyes of their own accord drawn to direct their vision at you,
in this briefest of interludes whilst my senses are free of stress.
Am I to be kidnapped from home, spirited away to these woods?
My motherland, goods and chattels, all acquaintance, family—gone?
Gone from the Forum, palestra, stadium, and gymnasia?
Miserable, miserable soul whose existence is mere grief,
what variant of human have I not metamorphosed into?
I am a woman, I am a young man, I am a juvenile, a boy,
I was the gymnasium's bloom, sweet-scented beauty:
mine were the doorways crowded out, mine were the doorsteps always warm,
mine were the bouquets of flowers which decorated the household,
as the sun climbed the heavens and I departed my bedroom.
Am I now reckoned slave to the gods, and in service to Cybele?
Am I considered a Maenad, am I half a self, am I unsexed?
Am I to lurk about the snowbound, evergreen slopes of chill Ida?
Am I sentenced to a lifetime beneath Phrygia's dizzy heights
where the deer finds its home in woods, where the wood-foraging boar lives?
Now, now I am agonised, now, now full of remorse.'

As soon as this speech was broadcast abroad, loud from her rosebud mouth,
conveying unexpected reports to the gods' acute hearing—
then Cybele untied the halter and reins binding her lions,
and provoking the master of herds, leashed on the left, she said:

'Go on,' she urged, 'go on angry beast, ensure insanity vex her,
see her downed by insanity, retreating to my wooded lands,
she who enjoys excess freedoms, over-eager to slip my hold.
Beat your hindquarters with your tail, bite back the trashing of yourself,
make sure every compass point is filled with your thundering roar
fearless one, unfurl your yellowy mane from your muscled neck.'

So Cybele furiously declared untying the halter,
the raging animal steeled, incited his angry being,
jumping up, growled out loudly, tramped down surrounding cover.
And as he approached the wetlands of glistening, foamy shore
and encountered effeminate Attis next to the marble sea,
he lunged. She, panicked and routed, a wild thing, retreated to woods:
always to stay, a life sentence, to be forever the slave-girl.

Goddess, great goddess, Cybebe, goddess, Matriarch of Dindymus,
pray all your discord and anger remain distant from my home—
push the rest to insanity, push the rest to pleasure's excess.

Toiling via numerous lands, over countless
  seas, I arrive, brother, with this last offering,
Final tokens which the dead carry with them,
  and mouth sayings above your mute remains
Hopelessly, as Fate stole away your living presence,
  my sad brother, heartlessly torn from me.
In any case, please accept these tokens I offer,
  as are handed over to those passed on.
Completely devastated with a brother's crying,
  to the end, brother, 'ave atque vale'.

——

These poems are from the complete translations
The Books of Catullus, forthcoming Carcanet, 2016

Busoni envelope flap courtesy Konrad Nowakowski

KONRAD NOWAKOWSKI

Busoni's Letter to Verdi

Late in his life, when Giuseppe Verdi had become a national institution, even pieces from his waste basket were preserved for collectors. A draft note of 1895, torn in half and pasted together later, illustrates this in a German Verdi catalogue of November 2013. Numbered "4420" in a corner sometime in the past, it came from an American antiquarian, who had offered it in a mixed catalogue in September 2013. The only other Verdi item in this mixed catalogue, numbered "4395" in pencil, was far cheaper—fewer words by Verdi—but not less attractive and is the one that concerns us here. Not meant to survive either, at least not by Verdi, it is a flap that he tore off an envelope in 1894. The small item bears Ferruccio Busoni's return address in Berlin and on the reverse, the only reason why it was saved, a short and banal but somehow delightful note by Verdi: "Piccolo Flacon / Colle Forte". A red wine of this name is still produced in the hilly region of Bardolino on the eastern banks of Lake Garda.

Verdi, an octogenarian by 1894, was more than fifty years older than his compatriot Busoni, who wrote his mature compositions and his *Sketch of a New Esthetic of Music* in the next century, after Verdi's death. The two composers stand for different eras, and the fragment that connects them in a double autograph seemed precious for that reason alone. As we will see, it also exposes an old error.

Busoni, his biographers tell us, had never had a high opinion of Italian opera and had not regarded Verdi as a great composer. But arriving in Berlin in April 1894, he went to see *Falstaff*, Verdi's late masterpiece, at the Court Opera, and this time he was overwhelmed. He began to draft a letter to Verdi, with whom he had not been in contact before, confessing that "*Falstaff* provoked in me such a revolution of spirit and feeling that I can with ample justification date the beginning of a new epoch in my artistic life from that time". The letter was to be accompanied by Busoni's newly published *Symphonic Tone Poem*, submitted for Verdi's appraisal, and it closed with these words:

> I tremble and hope: my heart will not rest until some sign has been sent from you. I dare not demand or beg you for a word. But, should you do me the honour of such a distinction, it would be a deed of inestimable goodness and would perhaps give me consolation and encouragement, fill me with self-confidence and enrich my insight.

Our flap was torn from the envelope of this letter but the books claim that the letter was not sent! Friedrich Schnapp found the Italian draft, now lost, after Busoni's death and published a German translation in the *Zeitschrift für Musik* in 1932, explaining in a note that the letter "was written in 1894 and never sent". Edward Dent, who like Schnapp was in close contact with Busoni's widow, elaborated on this in his Busoni biography of 1933: "To approach [Verdi] was a difficult matter; the sentences were written and re-written as if Busoni found himself a stranger to his native language. The letter was never finished and never dispatched." Since then, the draft has also been translated into English and re-translated into Italian from Schnapp's German translation, as the famous letter that Verdi never received from Busoni.

Thus, the flap is quite a surprise. The Berlin postmark must have been on the envelope's face but we can see that the letter, having crossed the Alps and the Apennines, reached Firenze Ferrovia on July 12, 1894 (the first of two overlapping postmarks). It crossed the Apennines again and passed through Borgo San Donnino, today's Fidenza, on July 13 (the second of the two overlapping postmarks), arriving at Busseto, where Verdi lived, the same day (the third postmark: "LUG" for July).

What could it have contained? The text that Schnapp translated in 1932, perhaps with further revisions but, because of the flap's small size, not the *Symphonic Tone Poem*, a score of almost a hundred pages. According to the draft, this was to "arrive together with this letter", which can be read as "under separate cover". Apparently it did, because it is still there in Verdi's villa, although unnoticed by Busoni experts. Not held in high esteem by Busoni in later years, the work was praised by Gustav Mahler and Max Reger when it was new but, as Sergio Sablich noted, it was "ispirata da un seguace di Wagner", Richard Strauss. What would Verdi have answered, Sablich asked, if letter and score had been sent? A response would not have vanished from Busoni's papers without ever having been mentioned to his wife, so the answer to Sablich's question seems to be: niente.

SOURCES

La Scala Autographs, Princeton, Fall 2013 Catalog, *Autographs, Photographs, Printed Music: Popular and Classical* (September).

Musikantiquariat Dr. Ulrich Drüner, Stuttgart, Katalog 71, *Giuseppe Verdi 1813–2013* (November 2013).

"Ferruccio Busoni: Brief an Giuseppe Verdi", aus dem italienischen Konzept übersetzt von Friedrich Schnapp, *Zeitschrift für Musik*, 99. Jahrgang, Heft 12, Dezember 1932, p. 1057.

Edward Joseph Dent, *Ferruccio Busoni: A Biography*, London: Oxford University Press, 1933.

Sergio Sablich, *Busoni*, Torino: EDT/Musica, 1982.

Ferruccio Busoni, *Selected Letters*, trans. & ed. Antony Beaumont, London: Faber, 1987.

Della Couling, *Ferruccio Busoni: "A Musical Ishmael"*, Oxford: Scarecrow, 2005.

http://www.rodoni.ch/busoni/busoniaverdi.html

http://www.rodoni.ch/busoni/cronologia/Note/notecrono936.html (Sablich)

Istituto Nazionale di Studi Verdiani, Parma, Biblioteca, emails of December 12, 2014 ("nel nostro archivio delle lettere verdiane non c'è traccia della corrispondenza in oggetto"), and January 9, 2015 ("in effetti una copia dell'op. 32a di Busoni si trova a Villa Verdi a Sant'Agata").

KONRAD NOWAKOWSKI

A SESSION IN HARLEM

THREE SKETCHES BY HAROLD LEHMAN

WHEN FORMER VIOLIN STUDENT, racing jockey, bandleader, and boxer Canada Lee, now an actor starring in *Big White Fog*, opened his Chicken Coop at 102 West 136th street in Harlem in November 1940, the *New York Amsterdam News* claimed that this had been the site of the Exclusive Club, where black male impersonator Gladys Bentley had sung her obscene songs eight years earlier. There was no reference to Bob Cole, an important black composer of the ragtime era, whose family had resided in this three-storey building before his suicide and for some time thereafter, at least until his mother's death in 1914. Cole's surviving partner in the team of Cole and Johnson, J. Rosamond Johnson, had been Lee's violin teacher and had shared the bill with Lee as an actor in *Mamba's Daughters* in 1939 and early 1940.

At Lee's Chicken Coop, the *New York Amsterdam News* wrote, Carol Boyd and Rollin Smith would appear "nitely, making it Harlem's only eating place with intimate entertainment". Smith, a singer and jazz saxophonist who spent much time in Europe, and Boyd had been in a trio with tenor vocalist Clarence Tisdale in 1934 and had now formed a vocal duo, singing "in 11 languages", as a somewhat later announcement claimed. There is no further documentation of their work at Lee's restaurant, and they were not mentioned in a report on its opening given by Dan Burley, star journalist at the *New York Amsterdam News*, in his famous column, "Back Door Stuff". Burley, who originated from Chicago, where bassist Milt Hinton had been one of his schoolmates, was a first-class blues pianist and, as a writer, one of the originators of "jive" language. At the opening, he wrote, he had "lamped" a number of stars and "oodles and oodles of fine greys", meaning whites.

Lee spent a great deal of money on his Chicken Coop, instead of earning anything from it, which only changed for a short while when he made news as Bigger Thomas in Orson Welles' stage production of *Native Son* by Richard Wright. He had just obtained this important role and was rehearsing it when a musical event with prominent guests took place at his Chicken Coop on March 2, 1941. Burley reported it in his column on March 8:

"Canada Lee's Coop popped Sunday evening, what with that fine blues and boogie woogie session cooked up by the Sepia Rhythm Club headed by Sam (Deep Elm St.) Price, Ralph (WNYC) Berton with the name, Dan Burley tacked on. Some 75 greys with a sprinkling of right-eous Harlemites jammed in to dig the proceedings dished up by yours truly, Price, Big Joe Turner, Pete (Boogie Woogie) Johnson and Margaret Bonds. So good was it that we'll repeat it, same place, same time (5 to 8:30) this coming Sabbath. Mildred Bailey, Eddie South, Eddie Morow [sic], Henrietta Flanner, Lawrence Richardson, Frances Williams and her hubby, Anthony Hill, and many other fine folks were there!!! It jumped, ole man!"

This is not quite in harmony with Mona Z. Smith's reference, in her biography of Lee, to the event as one in a series of "invitation-only jam sessions on Sunday mornings", where "highballs" would start "flowing at 10:00 or 11:00 a.m.". On March 15, Burley wrote that "Sam Price's blues sessions move to Jock's Place Sunday afternoon", and on March 22 he reported on "our Blues Session at Jock's Place on 7th Ave. Sunday p.m. [. . .] Sam Price, boogie-woogie king; Big Joe Turner and Huddie Ledbetter, plus Back Door [Burley] furnished the program which will be repeated with added names this Sunay [sic], 5 to 8, same place."

According to Burley, the event at the Chicken Coop on March 2 in-volved WNYC radio host Ralph Berton, who had held a first such session with Sam Price and others at the Newspaper Guild Club in October

1940, illustrating a lecture that he gave there on "Blues—Their Origin and Development". A similar session took place at the Ross Tavern in November, before Berton announced weekly Sunday sessions at the Village Vanguard in December 1940. Burley took part in one of these and was recorded on a "16-inch platter" (a large-format recording disc) by Berton, as the *New York Amsterdam News* proudly reported. But in mid-January 1941, Commodore Records' Milt Gabler started Sunday afternoon sessions at Ryan's, and the Berton parties at the Vanguard were discontinued soon thereafter.

On January 16, Berton devoted his radio show to Lionel Hampton, whose most recent records included the "Pig Foot Sonata", a piece that Hampton and Burley had written together. With a long and exhausting tour just behind him, Hampton was about to leave for the Grand Terrace in Chicago, from where he was expected to broadcast nationwide. Under the headline "Hampton to Terrace", the *New York Amsterdam News* claimed that he would use joint compositions by himself and Burley, including the "Sonata", in these broadcasts. In a feature article in the same issue, Burley praised Sam Price. Lincoln Day on February 12 brought Price and other participants of Berton's bashes to his WNYC studio for a broadcast that can now be listened to at www.wnyc.org, and on March 1, the day before the session at Lee's Chicken Coop, Berton's first lecture on "Jazz Appreciation" at the Metropolitan Music School seems to have dealt again with blues.

✳   ✳   ✳

Sixty years later, in April 2001, an internet search led me to three pencil drawings that had been made at the Chicken Coop on March 2, 1941. Five by eight inches in size, they were depicted on a website that Lisa Lehman Trager had devoted to the artist, Harold Lehman, her father. Lehman, born in October 1913, was eighty-seven years old at that time, but he was still active and took part in the correspondence that accom-

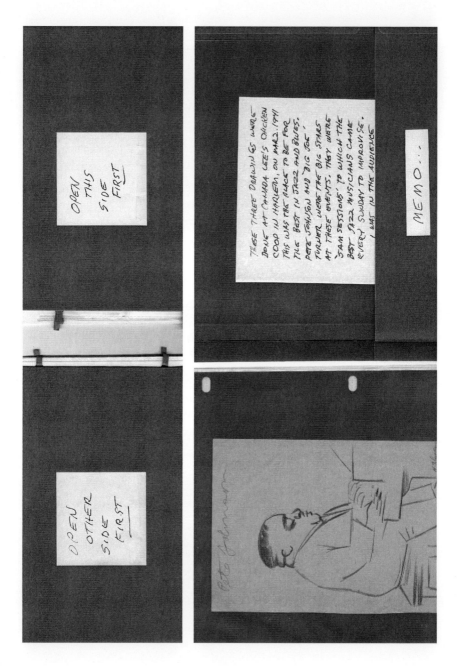

OPEN
THIS
SIDE
FIRST

OPEN
OTHER
SIDE
FIRST

THESE THREE DRAWINGS WERE
DONE AT CANADA LEE'S CHICKEN
COOP IN HARLEM, ON MAR 2 1941
THIS WAS THE PLACE TO BE FOR
THE BEST IN JAZZ AND BLUES.
PETE JOHNSON AND BIG JOE
TURNER WERE THE BIG STARS
AT THESE EVENTS. THEY WERE
"JAM SESSIONS" TO WHICH THE
BEST JAZZ MUSICIANS CAME
EVERY SUNDAY TO IMPROVISE.
(I WAS IN THIS AUDIENCE)

MEMO...

Pete Johnson

panied my purchase of the drawings. He had started his career as a sculptor before he switched to painting, working with Mexican muralist Siqueiros in 1932. When Siqueiros left Los Angeles, Lehman joined a group of Californian post-surrealists but in 1935 he moved to New York where he worked with Siqueiros again. Towards the end of the decade, he created the most important of his own murals, *Man's Daily Bread*, for the cafeteria at Riker's Island Penitentiary. Like many such works from the New Deal period, it has since been destroyed.

Lehman remembered the afternoon at Lee's Chicken Coop and described it in a memo, which accompanied the drawings to Vienna. He erred on one point: Dan Burley and Pete Johnson signed the sketches of themselves but Big Joe Turner, the most impressive of all blues shouters, endowed with a voice that remains unequalled, was illiterate and unable to write his name properly. "Big Joe Turner" in the sketch of him was clearly written by Pete Johnson. All three subjects were captured brilliantly in the sketches, with the one of Pete Johnson standing out as a piece of pure delight. Lehman sent them in a folder which, according to his instructions, has to be opened from the back, like a Hebrew or an Arabic book, in order to reveal the memo on the right and the Johnson drawing on top of the others on the left.

Excerpts from Lehman's emails of 2001

"Canada Lee's Chicken Coop was a famous jazz hangout during the period where jazz musicians would get together on Sundays to improvise and try out new gigs. I was invited to one of these and brought along a sketch pad. During the session, I made several drawings on the spot. The 'Pete Johnson' and the one of 'Big Joe Turner' are two of these. [. . .] Also present that same evening was Dan Burley. He was the m.c. that night . . . I made a drawing of him too holding the mike. All three autographed each of my drawings. I've preserved all three drawings for 60 years! [. . .] Now the astonishing part – after writing the above, Lisa called to tell me

about your latest e-mail message in which you tracked down the article by Dan Burley reviewing that very evening [. . .] I consider this whole episode an incredible happenstance – bordering on the occult. But if that's what it is, let's have more of them!!!" (May 5)

"I myself was one of the first American surrealists (in California 1933–35). I knew and admired the work of both Otto Dix and George Grosz as well as Max Pechstein, Paul Klee and the Bauhaus group. The Refregier murals you speak of [at Cafe Society Uptown] were very familiar to me – Ref (as we called him) was a very close friend of mine. We were both mural-painters on the WPA [Works Progress Administration] and in fact painted murals for the same building, the Riker's Island Penitentiary. So we were close personal friends and saw a lot of each other. [. . .] I can't close out without expressing my deep satisfaction at finding someone [. . .] who knows all of the above and really appreciates what [the drawings] signify. And in Austria yet!!! International culture is not dead!" (May 8)

"Well, the drawings are on their way [. . .] I wrapped them myself in as secure a manner as possible [. . .] Unroll the bubblewrap and you will find the photomailer. Inside this you will find 'The Holy Grail' – a blue album containing the drawings. [. . .] They are held in place only by surface tension of the protective plastic sheets and board stiffeners. You can keep them just as they are (as I did) or they can be matted and framed as we discussed previously [. . .] I hope you enjoy viewing the drawings as much as I enjoyed drawing them." (May 17)

"The Refregier clippings awoke memories long sleeping [. . .] Most of the work shown I saw at the time they were done. Especially interesting are the shots of the murals he did for Cafe Society Uptown [. . .] Incidentally – your two major interests in all this came together here since Pete Johnson and 'Big Joe' Turner performed regularly both Uptown and

THESE THREE DRAWINGS WERE
DONE AT CANADA LEE'S CHICKEN
COOP IN HARLEM, ON MAR 2. 1941
THIS WAS THE PLACE TO BE FOR
THE BEST IN JAZZ AND BLUES.
PETE JOHNSON AND `BIG JOE'
TURNER WERE THE BIG STARS
AT THESE EVENTS. THEY WERE
`JAM SESSIONS' TO WHICH THE
BEST JAZZ MUSICIANS CAME
EVERY SUNDAY TO IMPROVISE.
    I WAS IN THE AUDIENCE
THAT NIGHT WITH A SKETCH BOOK
AND DID THESE DRAWINGS ON
THE SPOT. THEY WERE NOT POSED
FOR. THEY WERE AUTOGRAPHED
BY EACH PERSON SHOWN AS WELL
AS BY ME THAT SAME EVENING.

MAY 15, 2001   H. Celender

[Cafe Society] Downtown, no doubt viewing the Uptown murals when they appeared there." (June 2)

A last message arrived in December 2002 on a computer print of an abstract watercolor by Lehman, with his handwritten wishes that it would find me "in good health and thriving in 2003". Harold Lehman, an unusually kind person in addition to his qualities as an artist, passed away in April 2006.

LITERATURE

Mona Z. Smith, *Becoming Something: The Story of Canada Lee*, New York: Faber and Faber, 2004.

New York Amsterdam News, February 22, 1933 (Gladys Bentley leaving the Exclusive Club); November 23 and 30, 1940 (opening of the Chicken Coop); January 11 and 25, 1941 (Burley at Vanguard, Hampton, Price); March 8, 15, and 22, 1941 (sessions at the Chicken Coop and at Jock's Place).

H.R.S. Society Rag, November 1940 and *Jazz Information*, October 25, 1940 to March 21, 1941 (reports on Berton and Gabler).

http://haroldlehman.com

ARTISTS & MUSICIANS AT THE

The previously unpublished photo on the following spread comes in an olive green Grand Terrace Cafe folder with the photo paper-framed inside right and autograph dedications to Mitch[ell Siporin] inside left. Musicians standing are Lionel Hampton left, Stuff Smith right, flanking Mexico-resident Guatemalan artist Carlos Mérida. Seated are WPA [Works Progress Administration] Federal Art Project Chicago artists and friends: Hal Bailey [status not established] ?–far left, Eula Long ?–2nd from right, and Fritz Long ?–far right, Edward Millman 4th from right, Mitchell Siporin 2nd from left, Lee Smith [née Helen Rogers] Stuff Smith's wife at the time ?–half-hidden. Three others, non-signing, are unidentified. The autograph dedications are in pencil except for those by Stuff Smith and Lee Smith in dark blue ink. The location is the Grand Terrace Cafe, Chicago, ?–late January or early February 1941.

Why will Stuff Smith see Mitch in St Louis? Edward Millman and Mitchell Siporin won a commission in 1939 to execute murals for St Louis Main Post Office. At first glance the photo might be taken to be a celebration of that, though not in 1939 or 1940. Work began fall 1941, completed June 1942. Smith was often based in Chicago at the time from where he toured, perhaps expecting to be in St Louis late 1941 or early 1942, though no notice has been found of his playing there precisely then. Hampton, on the other hand, was a visitor to Chicago. He was resident at the Grand Terrace Ballroom, opening 29 January 1941, closing 24 May 1941, while Smith opened in New York 24 April 1941, prior to which he was indisposed for some weeks. Part of a Chicago WGN studio jam session aircheck is extant dated 27 February 1941 with Smith, resident at Capitol Lounge, violin, Hampton vibes, Karl George trumpet and Vernon Alley bass both from Hampton's orchestra, and Teddy Wilson, resident at the Pump Room, piano. It can be heard on CD AB Fable ABCD1-015 *Stuff Smith, That Naughty Waltz*.

However, further consideration by Konrad Nowakowski shows more convincingly that the event is likely to be a farewell party for Carlos Mérida, organized by Mitchell Siporin, who is indeed described by Fritz Long in his dedication as "THE ORGANIZER". Mérida exhibited at the Katherine Kuh Gallery in Chicago on various occasions, including from the late 1930s to the early 1940s, during when Kuh and Mérida were lovers. He could, then, have visited Chicago at any time. It is curious that Kuh does not appear in the photo. She is not believed to be one of those who are unidentified.

GRAND TERRACE CAFE CHICAGO

Konrad Nowakowski's research suggests that the photograph may be associated with an exhibition mentioned in the *Chicago Daily Tribune*, 12 January 1941. On 21 January, PM listed a Merida [*sic*] exhibition at the Buchholz Gallery, New York, closing 8 February. On 26 January 1941, the *Chicago Daily Tribune* reported that a new exhibition would open at the Kuh Gallery on Tuesday, that is, 28 January. This must have been *Color in Modern Art*, as mentioned in the same paper on 9 February. On 19 February, the *Denton, Texas, Record-Chronicle* reported that Merida [*sic*] would join the faculty of North Texas State Teachers College on 1 April. It was reported that he was now in New York where he was exhibiting at the Buchholz Gallery, and that he would remain there until the exhibition closed, following which it would tour large museums elsewhere in the country, including St Louis and Los Angeles.

Mérida spoke several times of his friendships with musicians. In particular, in *Carlos Merida, Graphic Work, 1915–1981: Exhibition Tour* (Center for Inter-American Relations, New York, April 28–June 14, 1981): "I ceaselessly listen to music of the highest quality, especially piano. I have a weakness for hot jazz. I have managed to acquire an excellent collection of taped music of this kind. I have cultivated friendships with Stuff Smith, with Lionel Hampton and with Duke Ellington, and I am a profound admirer of Louis Armstrong. I would have very much liked to be a trumpet player at the Savoy."

Earlier, in *A Salute to Carlos Mérida: Catalog of the Exhibition, December 5, 1976–January 23, 1977* (University Art Museum, The University of Texas at Austin): "I made a point of meeting the greats of jazz when I was in the US. / Mugsy [*sic*: Muggsy] Spanier, the great trumpet player, was a very special friend of mine. Lionel Hampton and Stuff Smith also. With them, I learned everything about jazz. In reality, I would have liked better to be a good jazz trumpet player than a painter."

Reconciling what is known of the early 1941 Chicago residencies of Stuff Smith at Capitol Lounge and Lionel Hampton at Grand Terrace with Carlos Mérida's possible movements the photo would appear to be dated late January or early February 1941.

The folder was acquired in February 2014 by AB Fable Archive from Lusenhop Fine Art, who acquired it from Noah Hoffman, the son of Mitchell Siporin's sister, artist Shoshannah (Susanna Siporin Hoffman). She does not appear in the photo. There may well have been other prints, and autographed folders, for example, for Mérida.   AB

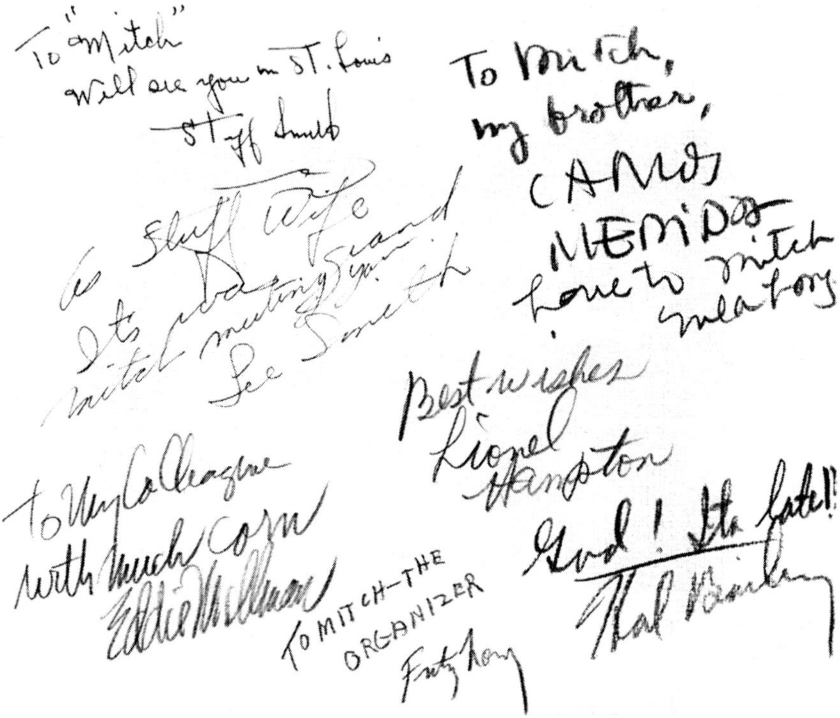

To "Mitch"
Will see you in St. Louis

To Mitch,
my brother,
CANDO
MEMIDOS
Love to Mitch

Best wishes
Lionel Hampton

To My Colleague
with much Corn
Eddie

To MITCH—THE
ORGANIZER

God! It's late!

Standing are orchestra leaders Lionel Hampton left and Stuff Smith right, flanking artist Carlos Mérida. Seated are artists and friends Hal Bailey ?–far left, Eula Long ?–2nd from right, Fritz Long ?–far right, Edward Millman 4th from right, Mitchell Siporin 2nd from left, Lee Smith, Stuff Smith's wife at the time, ?–half-hidden, and three others non-signing, unidentified. Grand Terrace Cafe, Chicago, ?–late January or early February 1941. Folder 250 x 165 mm, photo 166 x 114 mm, reproductions not to comparative scale.

DUCK BAKER is an American finger-style guitarist and composer based in England whose work ranges across the American and Irish tradition and such innovative composers as Herbie Nichols - http://duckbaker.com

GAIUS VALERIUS CATULLUS (*c.*84–54 BC) Roman poet, born ?Verona; Julius Caesar knew him; his brother died close to The Troad; his lover, Lesbia of the poems, was probably the powerful matriarch Clodia Metelli

CAROLINE CLARK is a poet from Lewes who has lived in Moscow and Montreal; her book *Saying Yes in Russian* appeared from Agenda in 2012; she has translated Olga Sedakova's "In Praise of Poetry", Open Letter, 2014

CHRISTINA CHALMERS is a poet and essayist born in Edinburgh who has spent time in Cambridge, Naples and Bologna and now lives in London; her work has appeared in *The Claudius App, Hi Zero, Dusie, No Prizes*

ERIKA DAGNINO is an Italian poet with a pamphlet in English, *Narcéte*, Propaganda, 2012; she also works with improvising musicians; the complete *I Canti dell'occhio* has twenty-four sections - www.erikadagnino.it

GUNNAR EKELÖF (1907–1968) Swedish poet and essayist, various translations of whose works are surveyed in Anthony Barnett, "Antonym: Gunnar Ekelöf's Table" in *Tears in the Fence*, 59, 2014

REI HAYAMA is a film and video maker living in Yokohama City whose other works include *A Castle Built Upside Down*, 2011, *Cinema of Stuffing*, 2010, and *A Child Goes Burying Dead Insects*, 2009 - www.reihayama.net

JASON KAO HWANG is a Chinese–American composer and improvising violinist based in New York whose other works include the opera *The Floating Box: A Story in Chinatown* - www.jasonkaohwang.com

PHILIPPE JACCOTTET is a Swiss poet who has lived in Grignan, France since the 1950s; in 2014 his work was added to the Bibliothèque de la Pléiade; his many translations include Hölderlin, Musil, Ungaretti

JASMINE JOHNSON is an artist moving between London and Delhi; her videos include *Thieves and Swindlers Are Not Allowed in Paradise*, 2014, *Compare Yourself*, 2013, *L. Making Pesto*, 2013; in progress *Third Party* is set in India

SOANDANG KIM YEON is a South Korean artist and calligrapher whose paintings frequently incorporate either quotations from classical Korean literature or her own legends

DOROTHY LEHANE is co-editor of *Litmus* a magazine exploring the interaction between poetry and science; her books are *Ephemeris*, Nine Arches, and *Places of Articulation*, dancing girl, both 2014 - www.litmuspublishing.co.uk

CEES NOOTEBOOM is a Dutch writer whose books include *Rituals, The Following Story, A Song of Truth and Semblance In the Dutch Mountains, Mokusei!, Roads to Berlin*, and *Letters to Poseidon*, Maclehose, 2014 - www.ceesnooteboom.com

KONRAD NOWAKOWSKI is a Viennese music researcher and the author of articles on piano blues, early jazz, and related matters

STEFANO PASTOR is an Italian violinist whose CDs include several on Slam; his sonority might be likened to alto or soprano sax or shakuhachi; he has collaborated with Erika Dagnino - www.stefanopastor.com

BRIDGET PENNEY is the author of *Index*, Book Works Semina series, 2008 and is currently working on a collection of short fiction in addition to the work represented here

YAMUPH PIKLÉ is a poet of undisclosed ethnos currently living in London and working in close collaboration with the poet and flautist Joseph Persad who contributed to *Snow 1*

PIERRE REVERDY (1889–1960) French poet, and intimate friend of Coco Chanel, whose translators into English have included Kenneth Rexroth, Ron Padgett, John Ashbery, and Ian Patterson in the AB review *Poetica*

ALEXANDRA SASHE is a Moscow-born poet, linguist and translator who spent many years living in Paris before settling in Vienna; her collection of poems *Antibodies* was published by Shearsman in 2013

CONCETTA SCOZZARO is an English poet currently living in Baltimore who has published a chapbook *Contrapposto Action Queen* Bad Press, 2013; her work has appeared in *Tripwire*, *Materials* and *The Claudius App*

SIMON SMITH is the author of *11781 W. Sunset Boulevard*, Shearsman, 2014, and chapbooks from Equipage and Oystercatcher, 2015; *New and Selected Poems* is forthcoming as is his editing of two books by Paul Blackburn

JØRN H SVÆREN is poet whose books include *Dronning av England*, Oslo, Kolon, 2011, and *Det ferdige verkets skjønnhet*, Stockholm, Chateaux, 2013; he edits an annual review *Den Engelske Kanal*; he contributed to *Snow 2*

BARRY SCHWABSKY is art crtic at *The Nation*; his books include *Words for Art*, Sternberg, Berlin, 2013, and the poetry collection *Trembling Hand Equilibrium* forthcoming from Black Square; he contributed to *Snow 2*

EMILIA TELESE is an Italian multimedia performance artist, often based in Brighton, now living in Coventry descended from 16th century philosopher and natural scientist Bernardino Telesio - www.emiliatelese.com

JOHN SEED is the author of *Manchester: August 16th & 17th 1819*, Intercapillary, 2013, and *Some Poems, 2006–12* Gratton/Shearsman, 2014; *Brandon Pithouse: Recollections of the Durham Coalfield* is forthcoming from Smokestack

YOLSKI is a Polish-born artist resident in Paris whose paintings include large scale architectural constructs; she has published *Trajectoirs de Pensée*, Bibliothèque Polonaise de Paris, 2014, *Formes, Signes et Trajectoires*, Yolski, 2005

ANDREA ZANZOTTO (1921–2011) Italian poet and essayist who also wrote texts for two films by Fellini translations of some of his poems appear in Anthony Barnett's collected *Translations*, 2012, and in *Snow 2*

Snow is grateful to Sung Hee Jin, Joe Luna, Aya Toraiwa and Naoko Toraiwa for their assistance

NOTE ABOUT NAMES

SNOW is inconsistent in printing names from languages in which the family name is placed first We follow the preferred form in this English context of the particular contributor so these are family names: Hayama, Jin, Kim, Kiuchi, Piklé, Toraiwa; Soandang is a name taken by Kim Yeon

NOTE ON STYLE

There are style differences between contributions in such matters as bibliographic citations or the use of single or double quotes so as to allow some leeway in personal preferences

SNOWB(O)ARD
ANTHONY BARNETT is the author of collected *Poems & and Translations*, both Tears in the Fence in assoc. Allardyce Book, 2012; he contributes critical "Antonyms" to the review *Tears in the Fence*; other books include bio-discographies of Stuff Smith and Eddie South, with violinistic CD series, and *Listening for Henry Crowder* who was Nancy Cunard's consort, 2007; *InExperience and UnCommon Sense in Translation*, 2014, is a pamphlet of a lecture, all Allardyce Book; work-in-progress is *A Disaccumulation of Knowledge* and *The Making of a Story*

IAN BRINTON is the editor of *A Manner of Utterance: The Poetry of J H Prynne*, Shearsman, 2009, *An Andrew Crozier Reader*, Carcanet, 2012, and Andrew Crozier, *Thrills and Frills: Selected Prose*, Shearsman, 2013 other books include *Contemporary Poetry: Poets and Poetry Since 1990*, CUP, 2009, and he is reviews editor at *Tears in the Fence*; his Ponge translations are published by Oystercatcher, 2015; he is writing a history of a school, so to speak, of Dulwich College-educated poets, and editing a 2016 Prynne 80th festschrift

FIONA ALLARDYCE
is an art restorer, specializing in frescos, who drew our snogo; she co-published the first collected volumes of J H Prynne, *Poems*, Andrew Crozier, *All Where Each Is* Douglas Oliver, *Kind*, and Veronica Forrest-Thomson, *Collected Poems and Translations*

The Sake Cup

SNOW NOTICES

AMY LI POSTSCRIPT TO SNOW 2
Snow 2 included "Requiem" for Amy Li. *Snow* is pleased to report that the company for which she worked as a safety engineer, DNV GL — Aberdeen — Oil & Gas, has established a memorial scholarship programme at University of Cambridge in her memory. The programme provides 50% funding to some 5 or 6 students who would otherwise be unable to pursue their studies over the course of their four-year degrees. Scholarships are awarded to undergraduates from any country outside the EU in the fields of Mathematics, Physics, Engineering or Chemical Engineering. DNV GL's contribution is matched by funding from the Cambridge Commonwealth, European & International Trust, which supports international students at the University. Amy attended Emmanuel College and the students may be there but not necessarily. In addition, Amy's colleagues at the company she previously worked for, UK Oil & Gas, have organized the planting of a tree and plaque in her memory at Victoria Park in Aberdeen

FORTHCOMING IN SNOW 4
An essay by Takashi Hiraide on the artist On Kawara translated by Kumiko Kiuchi